JOYCE'S THE DEAD

JOYCE'S THE DEAD

EDITED BY William T. Moynihan, University of Connecticut

ALLYN AND BACON, INC.   BOSTON, 1965

ALLYN AND BACON CASEBOOK SERIES

GENERAL EDITOR • LEONARD F. DEAN

© Copyright 1965 by Allyn and Bacon, Inc.
150 Tremont Street, Boston. All rights reserved.
No part of this book may be reproduced in any form,
by mimeograph, or any other means, without permission in
writing from the publisher.
Library of Congress Catalog Card Number: 65-18896
Printed in the United States of America

PREFACE

It may at first seem that so brief a work of fiction as "The Dead" does not require accounts of genesis, sources, correspondences, biography, or detailed commentary. Yet it seems unlikely that anyone who has tried to teach this story, tried to explain its subtleties of character and symbolism, will feel this way. And it is, in fact, the relative brevity of "The Dead" that makes the story ideally suited to meet the first requirement of controlled research—namely, that the research be *controlled*. Obviously, casebooks can be devised on larger subjects, but the larger the topic the more cumbersome the secondary material and the more unlikely it becomes that the student will accomplish any valid analysis, judgment, or evaluation.

There is always the danger in a literary casebook that the creative work will be buried beneath an avalanche of secondary material. But to object to the presence of secondary material is to misconceive the nature of the casebook. Such an objection wants the casebook to be something it is not—it wants the casebook to be creative rather than analytical. As Kenneth Burke acutely observes in his discussion of "The Dead," one should not expect criticism "to regive the quality of the story; for that one should go to the story itself."

The casebook method is, after all, a pedagogical device for encouraging students to think deeply and independently on complex and significant subjects. A literary casebook, more specifically, aims at introducing the student to some of the practices and pitfalls of literary criticism. It seeks to help him distinguish biography from fiction, fact from misconception, sensibility from stock response, informed insight from irresponsible commentary. "The Dead" and the criticism surrounding it admirably fulfill all of these ends.

This casebook depends for its organization (and implicitly for its worth) on three elements: the work itself, background materials, and critical interpretations.

Little need be said about the merits of Joyce's story. "The Dead" is almost universally acknowledged as one of the outstanding works of short fiction in this century. For R. W. B. Lewis, it is one of the stories which mark the beginning of modern literature.[1] It deals, as Allen Tate

[1] *The Picaresque Saint* (Philadelphia, 1959), p. 18.

says, with the "great contemporary subject: the isolation and frustration of personality." [2] In addition to its own brilliance and its importance to modern literature, "The Dead" is also an ideal introduction to the whole of Joyce's fiction and his techniques of symbolism. For, as Marvin Magalaner and Richard Kain note, "The Dead" represents Joyce's "most highly developed and artistic use of the short story medium and of symbols prior to *Ulysses*." [3]

All of Joyce's prose works involve some textual difficulties, and "The Dead" is no exception. Although not perfect, the 1914 Grant Richards and the 1916 B. W. Huebsch texts, which are the bases for subsequent editions, are essentially reliable. [4]

Literary meaning (like all verbal meaning) is a matter of contexts: the verbal contexts of the work itself, the context of the writer's life, the context of the writer's work and thought, the context of other literature that may have influenced the writer. The second section of this book, "the story in context," attempts to place "The Dead" in relation to Joyce's life, his other work, his thought, and the influence of other literature. Thus Part Two deals with Joyce's life during the time he was writing "The Dead," offers an account of Ibsen's germinal influence on Joyce, and examines "The Dead" as part of a collection of stories, *Dubliners*. One's understanding of any fiction by Joyce, furthermore, is aided by a knowledge of his working methods, his aesthetic, especially his concept of symbolism as embodied in his idea of "epiphany." (Considerable portions of three essays included in this text deal with Joyce's ideas on and uses of "epiphanies.")

What conclusion, finally, what judgment is one to draw about the meaning of this enigmatic story? All the necessary materials for analysis and comprehension, all the minute influences, sources and nuances of each work, the mind of Joyce himself, might be revealed to the reader, yet there would still be no guarantee of an intelligent judgment. Thus Part Three, "Critical Evaluations," proceeds by the practical, if sometimes fallible, method of presenting to the student five critical judgments by five scholars and teachers. Of course, the fact that these critical essays complement one another, supplement one another, contradict one another, emphasize and dismiss different aspects—all of these factors show

[2] *The Sewanee Review*, LVIII (Winter, 1950), p. 5.
[3] *Joyce: The Man, the Work, the Reputation* (Collier, N. Y., 1956), p. 102.
[4] For a detailed discussion of the textual history of "The Dead" see Robert E. Scholes, "Some Observations on the Text of *Dubliners*: 'The Dead'," *Studies in Bibliography*, XV (1962), pp. 191–205. In addition to codifying all the variant texts, Scholes lists the ten improvements Joyce made but which were never incorporated into the final text of *Dubliners*. Included among these improvements is Joyce's very significant change of "ghastly" to "ghostly" in this sentence near the end of the story: "A ghastly light from the streetlamp lay in a long shaft from one window to the door."

that the problem of judgment is a continuing problem. Each reader must re-examine the materials and the premises underlying his own and others' critical views. Just because the reader is exposed to five competent readings of a literary work does not mean that he can avoid the process of reaching his own conclusions. Just the opposite; it makes the process of reaching conclusions a more serious intellectual challenge. For the reader must not only judge the materials out of which the literary work grew, and distinguish the potential work from the actual work; he is finally required to decide which of various readings is best informed and convincing, or perhaps to decide why some judgments are not possible.

Any attempt to reach comprehensive conclusions about "The Dead" must eventually involve the work of critics. The critical analyses themselves must be appraised and evaluated. This, of course, is not a procedure peculiar to "The Dead," or to literature; it is a procedure common to all liberal education. The appraisal of opinions, ideas and reasons of others—especially when expressed in thoughtful discussion and writing —is, in fact, the essence of all education and what we loosely call "the democratic process." Thus, the final end of the student's examination of the critical writings on Joyce's story should not only be an increased appreciation and understanding of "The Dead," but a general sharpening of his critical and intellectual abilities.

Great literature, like Keats' "Urn," can "tease us out of thought/ As doth eternity," but the less lofty realm of analytical thought is the proper domain of controlled research. Analysis, understanding, judgment (or evaluation)—these are at the heart of the casebook method. And it is by emphasizing these intellectual endeavors that this text on "The Dead" seeks to prepare the student for more lofty literary experiences.

William T. Moynihan

CONTENTS

PART ONE

✸

✸

THE DEAD

THE DEAD*

Lily, the caretaker's daughter, was literally run off her feet. Hardly had she brought one gentleman into the little pantry behind the office on the ground floor and helped him off with his overcoat than the wheezy hall-door bell clanged again and she had to scamper along the bare hallway to let in another guest. It was well for her she had not to attend to the ladies also. But Miss Kate and Miss Julia had thought of that and had converted the bathroom upstairs into a ladies' dressing-room. Miss Kate and Miss Julia were there, gossiping and laughing and fussing, walking after each other to the head of the stairs, peering down over the banisters and calling down to Lily to ask her who had come.

It was always a great affair, the Misses Morkan's annual dance. Everybody who knew them came to it, members of the family, old friends of the family, the members of Julia's choir, any of Kate's pupils that were grown up enough, and even some of Mary Jane's pupils too. Never once had it fallen flat. For years and years it had gone off in splendid style, as long as anyone could remember; ever since Kate and Julia, after the death of their brother Pat, had left the house in Stoney Batter and taken Mary Jane, their only niece, to live with them in the dark, gaunt house on Usher's Island, the upper part of which they had rented from Mr. Fulham, the corn-factor on the ground floor. That was a good thirty years ago if it was a day. Mary Jane, who was then a little girl in short clothes, was now the main prop of the household, for she had the organ in Haddington Road. She had been through the Academy and gave a pupils' concert every year in the upper room of the Antient Concert Rooms. Many of her pupils belonged to the better-class families on the Kingstown and Dalkey line. Old as they were, her aunts also did their share. Julia, though she was quite grey, was still the leading soprano in Adam and Eve's, and Kate, being too feeble to go about much, gave music lessons to beginners on the old square piano in the back room. Lily, the caretaker's daughter, did housemaid's work for them. Though their life was modest, they believed in eating well; the best of everything: diamond-bone sirloins, three-shilling tea and the best bottled stout. But Lily seldom made a mistake in the orders, so that she got on well with her three mistresses. They were fussy, that was all. But the only thing they would not stand was back answers.

* From Dubliners by James Joyce. Originally published by B. W. Heubsch, Inc. in 1916. All rights reserved. By permission of The Viking Press, Inc.

Of course, they had good reason to be fussy on such a night. And then it was long after ten o'clock and yet there was no sign of Gabriel and his wife. Besides they were dreadfully afraid that Freddy Malins might turn up screwed. They would not wish for worlds that any of Mary Jane's pupils should see him under the influence; and when he was like that it was sometimes very had to manage him. Freddy Malins always came late, but they wondered what could be keeping Gabriel: and that was what brought them every two minutes to the banisters to ask Lily had Gabriel or Freddy come.

"O, Mr. Conroy," said Lily to Gabriel when she opened the door for him, "Miss Kate and Miss Julia thought you were never coming. Goodnight, Mrs. Conroy."

"I'll engage they did," said Gabriel, "but they forget that my wife here takes three mortal hours to dress herself."

He stood on the mat, scraping the snow from his goloshes, while Lily led his wife to the foot of the stairs and called out:

"Miss Kate, here's Mrs. Conroy."

Kate and Julia came toddling down the dark stairs at once. Both of them kissed Gabriel's wife, said she must be perished alive, and asked was Gabriel with her.

"Here I am as right as the mail, Aunt Kate! Go on up. I'll follow," called out Gabriel from the dark.

He continued scraping his feet vigorously while the three women went upstairs, laughing, to the ladies' dressing-room. A light fringe of snow lay like a cape on the shoulders of his overcoat and like toecaps on the toes of his goloshes; and, as the buttons of his overcoat slipped with a squeaking noise through the snow-stiffened frieze, a cold, fragrant air from out-of-doors escaped from crevices and folds.

"Is it snowing again, Mr. Conroy?" asked Lily.

She had preceded him into the pantry to help him off with his overcoat. Gabriel smiled at the three syllables she had given his surname and glanced at her. She was a slim, growing girl, pale in complexion and with hay-coloured hair. The gas in the pantry made her look still paler. Gabriel had known her when she was a child and used to sit on the lowest step nursing a rag doll.

"Yes, Lily," he answered, "and I think we're in for a night of it."

He looked up at the pantry ceiling, which was shaking with the stamping and shuffling of feet on the floor above, listened for a moment to the piano and then glanced at the girl, who was folding his overcoat carefully at the end of a shelf.

"Tell me, Lily," he said in a friendly tone, "do you still go to school?"

"O no, sir," she answered. "I'm done schooling this year and more."

"O, then," said Gabriel gaily, "I suppose we'll be going to your wedding one of these fine days with your young man, eh?"

The girl glanced back at him over her shoulder and said with great bitterness:

"The men that is now is only all palaver and what they can get out of you."

Gabriel coloured, as if he felt he had made a mistake and, without looking at her, kicked off his goloshes and flicked actively with his muffler at his patent-leather shoes.

He was a stout, tallish young man. The high colour of his cheeks pushed upwards even to his forehead, where it scattered itself in a few formless patches of pale red; and on his hairless face there scintillated restlessly the polished lenses and the bright gilt rims of the glasses which screened his delicate and restless eyes. His glossy black hair was parted in the middle and brushed in a long curve behind his ears where it curled slightly beneath the groove left by his hat.

When he had flicked lustre into his shoes he stood up and pulled his waistcoat down more tightly on his plump body. Then he took a coin rapidly from his pocket.

"O Lily," he said, thrusting it into her hands, "it's Christmas-time, isn't it? Just . . . here's a little. . . ."

He walked rapidly towards the door.

"O no, sir!" cried the girl, following him. "Really, sir, I wouldn't take it."

"Christmas-time! Christmas-time!" said Gabriel, almost trotting to the stairs and waving his hand to her in deprecation.

The girl, seeing that he had gained the stairs, called out after him: "Well, thank you, sir."

He waited outside the drawing-room door until the waltz should finish, listening to the skirts that swept against it and to the shuffling of feet. He was still discomposed by the girl's bitter and sudden retort. It had cast a gloom over him which he tried to dispel by arranging his cuffs and the bows of his tie. He then took from his waistcoat pocket a little paper and glanced at the headings he had made for his speech. He was undecided about the lines from Robert Browning, for he feared they would be above the heads of his hearers. Some quotation that they would recognise from Shakespeare or from the Melodies would be better. The indelicate clacking of the men's heels and the shuffling of their soles reminded him that their grade of culture differed from his. He would only make himself ridiculous by quoting poetry to them which they could not understand. They would think that he was airing his superior education. He would fail with them just as he had failed with the girl in the pantry. He had taken up a wrong tone. His whole speech was a mistake from first to last, an utter failure.

Just then his aunts and his wife came out of the ladies' dressing-room. His aunts were two small, plainly dressed old women. Aunt Julia was an inch or so the taller. Her hair, drawn low over the tops of her ears, was grey; and grey also, with darker shadows, was her large flaccid face. Though she was stout in build and stood erect, her slow eyes and parted lips gave her the appearance of a woman who did not know where she was or where she was going. Aunt Kate was more vivacious. Her face, healthier than her sister's, was all puckers and creases, like a shrivelled red apple, and her hair, braided in the same old-fashioned way, had not lost its ripe nut colour.

They both kissed Gabriel frankly. He was their favourite nephew, the son of their dead elder sister, Ellen, who had married T. J. Conroy of the Port and Docks.

"Gretta tells me you're not going to take a cab back to Monkstown tonight, Gabriel," said Aunt Kate.

"No," said Gabriel, turning to his wife, "we had quite enough of that last year, hadn't we? Don't you remember, Aunt Kate, what a cold Gretta got out of it? Cab windows rattling all the way, and the east wind blowing in after we passed Merrion. Very jolly it was. Gretta caught a dreadful cold."

Aunt Kate frowned severely and nodded her head at every word.

"Quite right, Gabriel, quite right," she said. "You can't be too careful."

"But as for Gretta there," said Gabriel, "she'd walk home in the snow if she were let."

Mrs. Conroy laughed.

"Don't mind him, Aunt Kate," she said. "He's really an awful bother, what with green shades for Tom's eyes at night and making him do the dumb-bells, and forcing Eva to eat the stirabout. The poor child! And she simply hates the sight of it! . . . O, but you'll never guess what he makes me wear now!"

She broke out into a peal of laughter and glanced at her husband, whose admiring and happy eyes had been wandering from her dress to her face and hair. The two aunts laughed heartily, too, for Gabriel's solicitude was a standing joke with them.

"Goloshes!" said Mrs. Conroy. "That's the latest. Whenever it's wet underfoot I must put on my goloshes. Tonight even, he wanted me to put them on, but I wouldn't. The next thing he'll buy me will be a diving suit."

Gabriel laughed nervously and patted his tie reassuringly, while Aunt Kate nearly doubled herself, so heartily did she enjoy the joke. The smile soon faded from Aunt Julia's face and her mirthless eyes were directed towards her nephew's face. After a pause she asked:

"And what are goloshes, Gabriel?"

"Goloshes, Julia!" exclaimed her sister. "Goodness me, don't you know what goloshes are? You wear them over your . . . over your boots, Gretta, isn't it?"

"Yes," said Mrs. Conroy. "Guttapercha things. We both have a pair now. Gabriel says everyone wears them on the Continent."

"O, on the Continent," murmured Aunt Julia, nodding her head slowly.

Gabriel knitted his brows and said, as if he were slightly angered:

"It's nothing very wonderful, but Gretta thinks it very funny because she says the word reminds her of Christy Minstrels."

"But tell me, Gabriel," said Aunt Kate, with brisk tact. "Of course, you've seen about the room. Gretta was saying . . ."

"O, the room is all right," replied Gabriel. "I've taken one in the Gresham."

"To be sure," said Aunt Kate, "by far the best thing to do. And the children, Gretta, you're not anxious about them?"

"O, for one night," said Mrs. Conroy. "Besides, Bessie will look after them."

"To be sure," said Aunt Kate again. "What a comfort it is to have a girl like that, one you can depend on! There's that Lily, I'm sure I don't know what has come over her lately. She's not the girl she was at all."

Gabriel was about to ask his aunt some questions on this point, but she broke off suddenly to gaze after her sister, who had wandered down the stairs and was craning her neck over the banisters.

"Now, I ask you," she said almost testily, "where is Julia going? Julia! Julia! Where are you going?"

Julia, who had gone halfway down one flight, came back and announced blandly: "Here's Freddy."

At the same moment a clapping of hands and a final flourish of the pianist told that the waltz had ended. The drawing-room door was opened from within and some couples came out. Aunt Kate drew Gabriel aside hurriedly and whispered into his ear:

"Slip down, Gabriel, like a good fellow and see if he's all right, and don't let him up if he's screwed. I'm sure he's screwed. I'm sure he is."

Gabriel went to the stairs and listened over the banisters. He could hear two persons talking in the pantry. Then he recognised Freddy Malins' laugh. He went down the stairs noisily.

"It's such a relief," said Aunt Kate to Mrs. Conroy, "that Gabriel is here. I always feel easier in my mind when he's here . . . Julia, there's Miss Daly and Miss Power will take some refreshment. Thanks for your beautiful waltz, Miss Daly. It made lovely time."

A tall wizen-faced man, with a stiff grizzled moustache and swarthy skin, who was passing out with his partner, said:

"And may we have some refreshment, too, Miss Morkan?"

"Julia," said Aunt Kate summarily, "and here's Mr. Browne and Miss Furlong. Take them in, Julia, with Miss Daly and Miss Power."

"I'm the man .for the ladies," said Mr. Browne, pursing his lips until his moustache bristled and smiling in all his wrinkles. "You know, Miss Morkan, the reason they are so fond of me is—"

He did not finish his sentence but, seeing that Aunt Kate was out of earshot, at once led the three young ladies into the back room. The middle of the room was occupied by two square tables placed end to end, and on these Aunt Julia and the caretaker were straightening and smoothing a large cloth. On the sideboard were arrayed dishes and plates, and glasses and bundles of knives and forks and spoons. The top of the closed square piano served also as a sideboard for viands and sweets. At a smaller sideboard in one corner two young men were standing, drinking hop-bitters.

Mr. Browne led his charges thither and invited them all, in jest, to some ladies' punch, hot, strong and sweet. As they said they never took anything strong, he opened three bottles of lemonade for them. Then he asked one of the young men to move aside, and, taking hold of the decanter, filled out for himself a goodly measure of whisky. The young men eyed him respectfully while he took a trial sip.

"God help me," he said, smiling, "it's the doctor's orders."

His wizened face broke into a broader smile, and the three young ladies laughed in musical echo to his pleasantry, swaying their bodies to and fro, with nervous jerks of their shoulders. The boldest said:

"O, now, Mr. Browne, I'm sure the doctor never ordered anything of the kind."

Mr. Browne took another sip of his whisky and said, with sidling mimicry:

"Well, you see, I'm like the famous Mrs. Cassidy, who is reported to have said: 'Now, Mary Grimes, if I don't take it, make me take it, for I feel I want it.' "

His hot face had leaned forward a little too confidentially and he had assumed a very low Dublin accent so that the young ladies, with one instinct, received his speech in silence. Miss Furlong, who was one of Mary Jane's pupils, asked Miss Daly what was the name of the pretty waltz she had played; and Mr. Browne, seeing that he was ignored, turned promptly to the two young men who were more appreciative.

A red-faced young woman, dressed in pansy, came into the room, excitedly clapping her hands and crying:

"Quadrilles! Quadrilles!"

Close on her heels came Aunt Kate, crying:

"Two gentlemen and three ladies, Mary Jane!"

"O, here's Mr. Bergin and Mr. Kerrigan," said Mary Jane. "Mr. Kerrigan, will you take Miss Power? Miss Furlong, may I get you a partner, Mr. Bergin. O, that'll just do now."

"Three ladies, Mary Jane," said Aunt Kate.

The two young gentlemen asked the ladies if they might have the pleasure, and Mary Jane turned to Miss Daly.

"O, Miss Daly, you're really awfully good, after playing for the last two dances, but really we're so short of ladies tonight."

"I don't mind in the least, Miss Morkan."

"But I've a nice partner for you, Mr. Bartell D'Arcy, the tenor. I'll get him to sing later on. All Dublin is raving about him."

"Lovely voice, lovely voice!" said Aunt Kate.

As the piano had twice begun the prelude to the first figure Mary Jane led her recruits quickly from the room. They had hardly gone when Aunt Julia wandered slowly into the room, looking behind her at something.

"What is the matter, Julia?" asked Aunt Kate anxiously. "Who is it?"

Julia, who was carrying in a column of table-napkins, turned to her sister and said, simply, as if the question had surprised her:

"It's only Freddy, Kate, and Gabriel with him."

In fact right behind her Gabriel could be seen piloting Freddy Malins across the landing. The latter, a young man of about forty, was of Gabriel's size and build, with very round shoulders. Her face was fleshy and pallid, touched with colour only at the thick hanging lobes of his ears and at the wide wings of his nose. He had coarse features, a blunt nose, a convex and receding brow, tumid and protruded lips. His heavy-lidded eyes and the disorder of his scanty hair made him look sleepy. He was laughing heartily in a high key at a story which he had been telling Gabriel on the stairs and at the same time rubbing the knuckles of his left fist backwards and forwards into his left eye.

"Good evening, Freddy," said Aunt Julia.

Freddy Malins bade the Misses Morkan good-evening in what seemed an offhand fashion by reason of the hibitual catch in his voice and then, seeing that Mr. Browne was grinning at him from the side-board, crossed the room on rather shaky legs and began to repeat in an undertone the story he had just told to Gabriel.

"He's not so bad, is he?" said Aunt Kate to Gabriel.

Gabriel's brows were dark but he raised them quickly and answered:

"O, no, hardly noticeable."

"Now, isn't he a terrible fellow!" she said. "And his poor mother made him take the pledge on New Year's Eve. But come on, Gabriel, into the drawing-room."

Before leaving the room with Gabriel she signalled to Mr. Browne by frowning and shaking her forefinger in warning to and fro. Mr. Browne nodded in answer and, when she had gone, said to Freddy Malins:

"Now, then, Teddy, I'm going to fill you out a good glass of lemonade just to buck you up."

Freddy Malins, who was nearing the climax of his story, waved the offer aside impatiently but Mr. Browne, having first called Freddy Malins' attention to a disarray in his dress, filled out and handed him a full glass of lemonade. Freddy Malins' left hand accepted the glass mechanically, his right hand being engaged in the mechanical readjustment of his dress. Mr. Browne, who face was once more wrinkling with mirth, poured out for himself a glass of whisky while Freddy Malins exploded, before he had well reached the climax of his story, in a kink of high-pitched bronchitic laughter and, setting down his untasted and overflowing glass, began to rub the knuckles of his left fist backwards and forwards into his left eye, repeating words of his last phrase as well as his fit of laughter would allow him.

> .   .   .   .

Gabriel could not listen while Mary Jane was playing her Academy piece, full of runs and difficult passages, to the hushed drawing-room. He liked music but the piece she was playing had no melody for him and he doubted whether it had any melody for the other listeners, though they had begged Mary Jane to play something. Four young men, who had come from the refreshment-room to stand in the doorway at the sound of the piano, had gone away quietly in couples after a few minutes. The only persons who seemed to follow the music were Mary Jane herself, her hands racing along the key-board or lifted from it at the pauses like those of a priestess in momentary imprecation, and Aunt Kate standing at her elbow to turn the page.

Gabriel's eyes, irritated by the floor, which glittered with beeswax under the heavy chandelier, wandered to the wall above the piano. A picture of the balcony scene in *Romeo and Juliet* hung there and beside it was a picture of the two murdered princes in the Tower which Aunt Julia had worked in red, blue and brown wools when she was a girl. Probably in the school they had gone to as girls that kind of work had been taught for one year. His mother had worked for him as a birthday present a waistcoat of purple tabinet, with little foxes' heads upon it, lined with brown satin and having round mulberry buttons. It was strange that his mother had had no musical talent though Aunt Kate used to call her the brains carrier of the Morkan family. Both she and Julia had always seemed a little proud of their serious and matronly sister. Her photograph stood before the pierglass. She held an open book on her knees and was pointing out something in it to Constantine who, dressed in a man-o'-war suit, lay at her feet. It was she who had chosen the names of her sons for she was very sensible of the dignity of family life. Thanks to her, Constantine was now senior curate in Balbriggan and, thanks to her, Gabriel himself had taken his degree in the Royal University. A shadow passed over his face as he remembered her sullen opposition to his marriage. Some slighting phrases she had used still rankled in his memory; she had once spoken of Gretta as being country cute and that was not true of Gretta at all. It was Gretta who had nursed her during all her last long illness in their house at Monkstown.

He knew that Mary Jane must be near the end of her piece for she was playing again the opening melody with runs of scales after every bar and while he waited for the end the resentment died down in his heart. The piece ended with a trill of octaves in the treble and a final deep octave in the bass. Great applause greeted Mary Jane as, blushing and rolling up her music nervously, she escaped from the room. The most vigorous clapping came from the four young men in the doorway who had gone away to the refreshment-room at the beginning of the piece but had come back when the piano had stopped.

Lancers were arranged. Gabriel found himself partnered with Miss Ivors. She was a frank-mannered talkative young lady, with a freckled face and prominent brown eyes. She did not wear a low-cut bodice and the large brooch which was fixed in the front of her collar bore on it an Irish device and motto.

When they had taken their places she said abruptly:

"I have a crow to pluck with you."

"With me?" said Gabriel.

She nodded her head gravely.

"What is it?" asked Gabriel, smiling at her solemn manner.

"Who is G. C.?" answered Miss Ivors, turning her eyes upon him.

Gabriel coloured and was about to knit his brows, as if he did not understand, when she said bluntly:

"O, innocent Amy! I have found out that you write for *The Daily Express*. Now, aren't you ashamed of yourself?"

"Why should I be ashamed of myself?" asked Gabriel, blinking his eyes and trying to smile.

"Well, I'm ashamed of you," said Miss Ivors frankly. "To say you'd write for a paper like that. I didn't think you were a West Briton."

A look of perplexity appeared on Gabriel's face. It was true that he wrote a literary column every Wednesday in *The Daily Express*, for which he was paid fifteen shillings. But that did not make him a West Briton surely. The books he received for review were almost more welcome than the paltry cheque. He loved to feel the covers and turn over the pages of newly printed books. Nearly every day when his teaching in the college was ended he used to wander down the quays to the second-hand booksellers, to Hickey's on Bachelor's Walk, to Webb's or Massey's on Aston's Quay, or to O'Clohissey's in the by-street. He did not know how to meet her charge. He wanted to say that literature was above politics. But they were friends of many years' standing and their careers had been parallel, first at the University and then as teachers: he could not risk a grandiose phrase with her. He continued blinking his eyes and trying to smile and murmured lamely that he saw nothing political in writing reviews of books.

When their turn to cross had come he was still perplexed and inattentive. Miss Ivors promptly took his hand in a warm grasp and said in a soft friendly tone:

"Of course, I was only joking. Come, we cross now."

When they were together again she spoke of the University question and Gabriel felt more at ease. A friend of hers had shown her his review of Browning's poems. That was how she had found out the secret: but she liked the review immensely. Then she said suddenly:

"O, Mr. Conroy, will you come for an excursion to the Aran Isles this summer? We're going to stay there a whole month. It will be splendid out in the Atlantic. You ought to come. Mr. Clancy is coming, and Mr. Kilkelly and Kathleen Kearney. It would be splendid for Gretta too if she'd come. She's from Connacht, isn't she?"

"Her people are," said Gabriel shortly.

"But you will come, won't you?" said Miss Ivors, laying her warm hand eagerly on his arm.

"The fact is," said Gabriel, "I have just arranged to go—"

"Go where?" asked Miss Ivors.

"Well, you know, every year I go for a cycling tour with some fellows and so—"

"But where?" asked Miss Ivors.

"Well, we usually go to France or Belgium or perhaps Germany," said Gabriel awkwardly.

"And why do you go to France and Belgium," said Miss Ivors, "instead of visiting your own land?"

"Well," said Gabriel, "it's partly to keep in touch with the languages and partly for a change."

"And haven't you your own language to keep in touch with—Irish?" asked Miss Ivors.

"Well," said Gabriel, "if it comes to that, you know, Irish is not my language."

Their neighbours had turned to listen to the cross-examination. Gabriel glanced right and left nervously and tried to keep his good humour under the ordeal which was making a blush invade his forehead.

"And haven't you your own land to visit," continued Miss Ivors, "that you know nothing of, your own people, and your own country?"

"O, to tell you the truth," retorted Gabriel suddenly, "I'm sick of my own country, sick of it!"

"Why?" asked Miss Ivors.

Gabriel did not answer for his retort had heated him.

"Why?" repeated Miss Ivors.

They had to go visiting together and, as he had not answered her, Miss Ivors said warmly:

"Of course, you've no answer."

Gabriel tried to cover his agitation by taking part in the dance with great energy. He avoided her eyes for he had seen a sour expression on her face. But when they met in the long chain he was surprised to feel his hand firmly pressed. She looked at him from under her brows for a moment quizzically until he smiled. Then, just as the chain was about to start again, she stood on tiptoe and whispered into his ear:

"West Briton!"

When the lancers were over Gabriel went away to a remote corner of the room where Freddy Malins' mother was sitting. She was a stout feeble old woman with white hair. Her voice had a catch in it like her son's and she stuttered slightly. She had been told that Freddy had come and that he was nearly all right. Gabriel asked her whether she had had a good crossing. She lived with her married daughter in Glasgow and came to Dublin on a visit once a year. She answered placidly that she had had a beautiful crossing and that the captain had been most attentive to her. She spoke also of the beautiful house her daughter kept in Glasgow, and of all the friends they had there. While her tongue rambled on Gabriel tried to banish from his mind all memory of the unpleasant incident with Miss Ivors. Of course the girl or woman, or whatever she was, was an enthusiast but there was a time for all things. Perhaps he ought not to have answered her like that. But she had no right to call him a West Briton before people, even in joke. She had tried to make him ridiculous before people, heckling him and staring at him with her rabbit's eyes.

He saw his wife making her way towards him through the waltzing couples. When she reached him she said into his ear:

"Gabriel, Aunt Kate wants to know won't you carve the goose as usual. Miss Daly will carve the ham and I'll do the pudding."

"All right," said Gabriel.

"She's sending in the younger ones first as soon as this waltz is over so that we'll have the table to ourselves."

"Were you dancing?" asked Gabriel.

"Of course I was. Didn't you see me? What row had you with Molly Ivors?"

"No row. Why? Did she say so?"

"Something like that. I'm trying to get that Mr. D'Arcy to sing. He's full of conceit, I think."

"There was no row," said Gabriel moodily, "only she wanted me to go for a trip to the west of Ireland and I said I wouldn't."

His wife clasped her hands excitedly and gave a little jump.

"O, do go, Gabriel," she cried. "I'd love to see Galway again."

"You can go if you like," said Gabriel coldly.

She looked at him for a moment, then turned to Mrs. Malins and said:

"There's a nice husband for you, Mrs. Malins."

While she was threading her way back across the room Mrs. Malins, without adverting to the interruption, went on to tell Gabriel what beautiful places there were in Scotland and beautiful scenery. Her son-in-law brought them every year to the lakes and they used to go fishing. Her son-in-law was a splendid fisher. One day he caught a beautiful big fish and the man in the hotel cooked it for their dinner.

Gabriel hardly heard what she said. Now that supper was coming near he began to think again about his speech and about the quotation. When he saw Freddy Malins coming across the room to visit his mother Gabriel left the chair free for him and retired into the embrasure of the window. The room had already cleared and from the back room came the clatter of plates and knives. Those who still remained in the drawing-room seemed tired of dancing and were conversing quietly in little groups. Gabriel's warm trembling fingers tapped the cold pane of the window. How cool it must be outside! How pleasant it would be to walk out alone, first along by the river and then through the park! The snow would be lying on the branches of the trees and forming a bright cap on the top of the Wellington Monument. How much more pleasant it would be there than at the supper-table!

He ran over the headings of his speech: Irish hospitality, sad memories, the Three Graces, Paris, the quotation from Browning. He repeated to himself a phrase he had written in his review: "One feels that one is listening to a thought-tormented music." Miss Ivors had praised the review. Was she sincere? Had she really any life of her own behind all her propagandism? There had never been any ill-feeling between them until that night. It unnerved him to think that she would be at the supper-table, looking up at him while he spoke with her critical quizzing eyes. Perhaps she would not be sorry to see him fail in his speech. An idea came into his mind and gave him courage. He would say, alluding to Aunt Kate and Aunt Julia: "Ladies and Gentlemen, the generation which is now on the wane among us may have had its faults but for my part I think it had certain qualities of hospitality, of humour, of humanity, which the new and very serious and hypereducated generation that is growing up around us seems to me to lack." Very good: that was one for Miss Ivors. What did he care that his aunts were only two ignorant old women?

A murmur in the room attracted his attention. Mr. Browne was advancing from the door, gallantly escorting Aunt Julia, who leaned upon his arm, smiling and hanging her head. An irregular musketry of applause escorted her also as far as the piano and then, as Mary Jane seated herself on the stool, and Aunt Julia, no longer smiling, half turned so as to pitch her voice fairly into the room, gradually ceased. Gabriel recognised the prelude. It was that of an old song of Aunt Julia's— *Arrayed for the Bridal*. Her voice, strong and clear in tone, attacked with great spirit the runs which embellish the air and though she sang very rapidly she did not miss even the smallest of the grace notes. To follow the voice, without looking at the singer's face, was to feel and share the excitement of swift and secure flight. Gabriel applauded loudly with all the others at the close of the song and loud applause was borne in from the invisible supper-table. It sounded so genuine that a little colour struggled into Aunt Julia's face as she bent to replace in the music-stand the old leather-bound song-book that had her initials on the cover. Freddy Malins, who had listened with his head perched sideways to hear her better, was still applauding when everyone else had ceased and talking animatedly to his mother who nodded her head gravely and slowly in acquiescence. At last, when he could clap no more, he stood up suddenly and hurried across the room to Aunt Julia whose hand he seized and held in both his hands, shaking it when words failed him or the catch in his voice proved too much for him.

"I was just telling my mother," he said, "I never heard you sing so well, never. No, I never heard your voice so good as it is tonight. Now! Would you believe that now? That's the truth. Upon my word and honour that's the truth. I never heard your voice sound so fresh and so . . . so clear and fresh, never."

Aunt Julia smiled broadly and murmured something about compliments as she released her hand from his grasp. Mr. Browne extended his open hand towards her and said to those who were near him in the manner of a showman introducing a prodigy to an audience:

"Miss Julia Morkan, my latest discovery!"

He was laughing very heartily at this himself when Freddy Malins turned to him and said:

"Well, Browne, if you're serious you might make a worse discovery. All I can say is I never heard her sing half so well as long as I am coming here. And that's the honest truth."

"Neither did I," said Mr. Browne. "I think her voice has greatly improved."

Aunt Julia shrugged her shoulders and said with meek pride:

"Thirty years ago I hadn't a bad voice as voices go."

"I often told Julia," said Aunt Kate emphatically, "that she was simply thrown away in that choir. But she never would be said by me."

She turned as if to appeal to the good sense of the others against a refractory child while Aunt Julia gazed in front of her, a vague smile of reminiscence playing on her face.

"No," continued Aunt Kate, "she wouldn't be said or led by anyone, slaving there in that choir night and day, night and day. Six o'clock on Christmas morning! And all for what?"

"Well, isn't it for the honour of God, Aunt Kate?" asked Mary Jane, twisting round on the piano-stool and smiling.

Aunt Kate turned fiercely on her niece and said:

"I know all about the honour of God, Mary Jane, but I think it's not at all honourable for the pope to turn out the women out of the choirs that have slaved there all their lives and put little whipper-snappers of boys over their heads. I suppose it is for the good of the Church if the pope does it. But it's not just, Mary Jane, and it's not right."

She had worked herself into a passion and would have continued in defence of her sister for it was a sore subject with her but Mary Jane, seeing that all the dancers had come back, intervened pacifically:

"Now, Aunt Kate, you're giving scandal to Mr. Browne who is of the other persuasion."

Aunt Kate turned to Mr. Browne, who was grinning at this allusion to his religion, and said hastily:

"O, I don't question the pope's being right. I'm only a stupid old woman and I wouldn't presume to do such a thing. But there's such a thing as common everyday politeness and gratitude. And if I were in Julia's place I'd tell that Farther Healey straight up to his face . . ."

"And besides, Aunt Kate," said Mary Jane, "we really are all hungry and when we are hungry we are all very quarrelsome."

"And when we are thirsty we are also quarrelsome," added Mr. Browne.

"So that we had better go to supper," said Mary Jane, "and finish the discussion afterwards."

On the landing outside the drawing-room Gabriel found his wife and Mary Jane trying to persuade Miss Ivors to stay for supper. But Miss Ivors, who had put on her hat and was buttoning her cloak, would not stay. She did not feel in the least hungry and she had already overstayed her time.

"But only for ten minutes, Molly," said Mrs. Conroy. "That won't delay you."

"To take a pick itself," said Mary Jane, "after all your dancing."

"I really couldn't," said Miss Ivors.

"I am afraid you didn't enjoy yourself at all," said Mary Jane hopelessly.

"Ever so much, I assure you," said Miss Ivors, "but you really must let me run off now."

"But how can you get home?" asked Mrs. Conroy.

"O, it's only two steps up the quay."

Gabriel hesitated a moment and said:

"If you will allow me, Miss Ivors, I'll see you home if you are really obliged to go."

But Miss Ivors broke away from them.

"I won't hear of it," she cried. "For goodness' sake go in to your suppers and don't mind me. I'm quite well able to take care of myself."

"Well, you're the comical girl, Molly," said Mrs. Conroy frankly.

"*Beannacht libh*," cried Miss Ivors, with a laugh, as she ran down the staircase.

Mary Jane gazed after her, a moody puzzled expression on her face, while Mrs. Conroy learned over the banisters to listen for the hall-door. Gabriel asked himself was he the cause of her abrupt departure. But she did not seem to be in ill humour: she had gone away laughing. He stared blankly down the staircase.

At the moment Aunt Kate came toddling out of the supper-room, almost wringing her hands in despair.

"Where is Gabriel?" she cried. "Where on earth is Gabriel? There's everyone waiting in there, stage to let, and nobody to carve the goose!"

"Here I am, Aunt Kate!" cried Gabriel, with sudden animation, "ready to carve a flock of geese, if necessary."

A fat brown goose lay at one end of the table and at the other end, on a bed of creased paper strewn with sprigs of parsely, lay a great ham, stripped of its outer skin and peppered over with crust crumbs, a neat paper frill round its shin and beside this was a round of spiced beef. Between these rival ends ran parallel lines of side-dishes: two little minsters of jelly, red and yellow; a shallow dish full of blocks of blancmange and red jam, a large green leaf-shaped dish with a stalk-shaped handle, on which lay bunches of purple raisins and peeled almonds, a companion dish on which lay a solid rectangle of Smyrna figs, a dish of custard topped with grated nutmeg, a small bowl full of chocolates and sweets wrapped in gold and silver papers and a glass vase in which stood some tall celery stalks. In the centre of the table there stood, as sentries to a fruit-stand which upheld a pyramid of oranges and American apples, two squat old-fashioned decanters of cut glass, one containing port and the other dark sherry. On the closed square piano a pudding in a huge yellow dish lay in waiting and behind it were three squads of bottles of stout and ale and minerals, drawn up according to the colours of their uniforms, the first two black, with brown and red labels, the third and smallest squad white, with transverse green sashes.

Gabriel took his seat boldly at the head of the table and, having looked to the edge of the carver, plunged his fork firmly into the goose. He felt quite at ease now for he was an expert carver and liked nothing better than to find himself at the head of a well-laden table.

"Miss Furlong, what shall I send you?" he asked. "A wing or a slice of the breast?"

"Just a small slice of the breast."

"Miss Higgins, what for you?"

"O, anything at all, Mr. Conroy."

While Gabriel and Miss Daly exchanged plates of goose and plates of ham and spiced beef Lily went from guest to guest with a dish of hot floury potatoes wrapped in a white napkin. This was Mary Jane's idea and she had also suggested apple sauce for the goose but Aunt Kate had said that plain roast goose without any apple sauce had always been good enough for her and she hoped she might never eat worse. Mary Jane waited on her pupils and saw that they got the best slices and Aunt Kate and Aunt Julia opened and carried across from the piano bottles of stout and ale for the gentlemen and bottles of minerals for the ladies. There was a great deal of confusion and laughter and noise, the noise of orders and counter-orders, of knives and forks, of corks and glass-stoppers. Gabriel began to carve second helpings as soon as he had finshed the first round without serving himself. Everyone protested loudly so that he compromised by taking a long draught of stout for he had found the carving hot work. Mary Jane settled down quietly to her supper but Aunt Kate and Aunt Julia were still toddling round the table, walking on each other's heels, getting in each other's way and giving each other unheeded orders. Mr. Browne begged of them to sit down and eat their suppers and so did Gabriel but they said there was time enough, so that, at last, Freddy Malins stood up and, capturing Aunt Kate, plumped her down on her chair amid general laughter.

When everyone had been well served Gabriel said, smiling:

"Now, if anyone wants a little more of what vulgar people call stuffing let him or her speak."

A chorus of voices invited him to begin his own supper and Lily came forward with three potatoes which she had reserved for him.

"Very well," said Gabriel amiably, as he took another preparatory draught, "kindly forget my existence, ladies and gentlemen, for a few minutes."

He set to his supper and took no part in the conversation with which the table covered Lily's removal of the plates. The subject of talk was the opera company which was then at the Theatre Royal. Mr. Bartell D'Arcy, the tenor, a dark-complexioned young man with a smart moustache, praised very highly the leading contralto of the company but Miss Furlong thought she had a rather vulgar style of production. Freddy Malins said there was a Negro chieftain singing in the second part of the Gaiety pantomime who had one of the finest tenor voices he had ever heard.

"Have you heard him?" he asked Mr. Bartell D'Arcy across the table.

"No," answered Mr. Bartell D'Arcy carelessly.

"Because," Freddy Malins explained, "now I'd be curious to hear your opinion of him. I think he has a grand voice."

"It takes Teddy to find out the really good things," said Mr. Browne familiarly to the table.

"And why couldn't he have a voice too?" asked Freddy Malins sharply. "Is it because he's only a black?"

Nobody answered this question and Mary Jane led the table back to the legitimate opera. One of her pupils had given her a pass for *Mignon.* Of course it was very fine, she said, but it made her think of poor Georgina Burns. Mr. Browne could go back farther still, to the old Italian companies that used to come to Dublin—Tietjens, Ilma de Murzka, Campanini, the great Trebelli, Giuglini, Ravelli, Aramburo. Those were the days, he said, when there was something like singing to be heard in Dublin. He told too of how the top gallery of the old Royal used to be packed night after night, of how one night an Italian tenor had sung five encores to *Let me like a Soldier fall*, introducing a high C every time, and of how the gallery boys would sometimes in their enthusiasm unyoke the horses from the carriage of some great *prima donna* and pull her themselves through the streets to her hotel. Why did they never play the grand old operas now, he asked, *Dinorah, Lucrezia Borgia*? Because they could not get the voices to sing them: that was why.

"O, well," said Mr. Bartell D'Arcy, "I presume there are as good singers today as there were then."

"Where are they?" asked Mr. Browne defiantly.

"In London, Paris, Milan," said Mr. Bartell D'Arcy warmly. "I suppose Caruso, for example, is quite as good, if not better than any of the men you have mentioned."

"Maybe so," said Mr. Browne. "But I may tell you I doubt it strongly."

"O, I'd give anything to hear Caruso sing," said Mary Jane.

"For me," said Aunt Kate, who had been picking a bone, "there was only one tenor. To please me, I mean. But I suppose none of you ever heard of him."

"Who was he, Miss Morkan?" asked Mr. Bartell D'Arcy politely.

"His name," said Aunt Kate, "was Parkinson. I heard him when he was in his prime and I think he had then the purest tenor voice that was ever put into a man's throat."

"Strange," said Mr. Bartell D'Arcy. "I never even heard of him."

"Yes, yes, Miss Morkan is right," said Mr. Browne. "I remember hearing of old Parkinson but he's too far back for me."

"A beautiful, pure, sweet, mellow English tenor," said Aunt Kate with enthusiasm.

Gabriel having finished, the huge pudding was transferred to the table. The clatter of forks and spoons began again. Gabriel's wife served out spoonfuls of the pudding and passed the plates down the table. Midway down they were held up by Mary Jane, who replenished them with raspberry or orange jelly or with blancmange and jam. The pudding was of Aunt Julia's making and she received praises for it from all quarters. She herself said that it was not quite brown enough.

"Well, I hope, Miss Morkan," said Mr. Browne, "that I'm brown enough for you because, you know, I'm all brown."

All the gentlemen, except Gabriel, ate some of the pudding out of compliment to Aunt Julia. As Gabriel never ate sweets the celery had been left for him. Freddy Malins also took a stalk of celery and ate it with his pudding. He had been told that celery was a capital thing for the blood and he was just then under doctor's care. Mrs. Malins, who had been silent all through the supper, said that her son was going down to Mount Melleray in a week or so. The table then spoke of Mount Melleray, how bracing the air was down there, how hospitable the monks were and how they never asked for a penny-piece from their guests.

"And do you mean to say," asked Mr. Browne incredulously, "that a chap can go down there and put up there as if it were a hotel and live on the fat of the land and then come away without paying anything?"

"O, most people give some donation to the monastery when they leave," said Mary Jane.

"I wish we had an institution like that in our Church," said Mr. Browne candidly.

He was astonished to hear that the monks never spoke, got up at two in the morning and slept in their coffins. He asked what they did it for.

"That's the rule of the order," said Aunt Kate firmly.

"Yes, but why?" asked Mr. Browne.

Aunt Kate repeated that it was the rule, that was all. Mr. Browne still seemed not to understand. Freddy Malins explained to him, as best he could, that the monks were trying to make up for the sins committed by all the sinners in the outside world. The explanation was not very clear for Mr. Browne grinned and said:

"I like that idea very much but wouldn't a comfortable spring bed do them as well as a coffin?"

"The coffin," said Mary Jane, "is to remind them of their last end."

As the subject had grown lugubrious it was buried in a silence of the table during which Mrs. Malins could be heard saying to her neighbour in an indistinct undertone:

"They are very good men, the monks, very pious men."

The raisins and almonds and figs and apples and oranges and chocolates and sweets were now passed about the table and Aunt Julia invited all the guests to have either port or sherry. At first Mr. Bartell D'Arcy refused to take either but one of his neighbours nudged him and whispered something to him upon which he allowed his glass to be filled. Gradually as the last glasses were being filled the conversation ceased. A pause followed, broken only by the noise of the wine and by unsettlings of chairs. The Misses Morkan, all three, looked down at the tablecloth. Someone coughed once or twice and then a few gentlemen patted the table gently as a signal for silence. The silence came and Gabriel pushed back his chair and stood up.

The patting at once grew louder in encouragement and then ceased altogether. Gabriel leaned his ten trembling fingers on the tablecloth and smiled nervously at the company. Meeting a row of upturned faces he raised his eyes to the chandelier. The piano was playing a waltz tune

and he could hear the skirts sweeping against the drawing-room door.
People, perhaps, were standing in the snow on the quay outside, gazing
up at the lighted windows and listening to the waltz music. The air was
pure there. In the distance lay the park where the trees were weighted
with snow. The Wellington Monument wore a gleaming cap of snow that
flashed westward over the white field of Fifteen Acres.

He began:

"Ladies and Gentlemen,

"It has fallen to my lot this evening, as in years past, to perform a
very pleasing task but a task for which I am afraid my poor powers as
a speaker are all too inadequate."

"No, no!" said Mr. Browne.

"But, however that may be, I can only ask you tonight to take the
will for the deed and to lend me your attention for a few moments
while I endeavour to express to you in words what my feelings are on
this occasion.

"Ladies and Gentlemen, it is not the first time that we have gathered
together under this hospitable roof, around this hospitable board. It is
not the first time that we have been the recipients—or perhaps, I had
better say, the victims—of the hospitality of certain good ladies."

He made a circle in the air with his arm and paused. Everyone
laughed or smiled at Aunt Kate and Aunt Julia and Mary Jane who all
turned crimson with pleasure. Gabriel went on more boldly:

"I feel more strongly with every recurring year that our country has
no tradition which does it so much honour and which is should guard
so jealously as that of its hospitality. It is a tradition that is unique as
far as my experience goes (and I have visited not a few places abroad)
among the modern nations. Some would say, perhaps, that with us it is
rather a failing than anything to be boasted of. But granted even that, it
is, to my mind, a princely failing, and one that I trust will long be cultivated among us. Of one thing, at least, I am sure. As long as this one
roof shelters the good ladies aforesaid—and I wish from my heart it
may do so for many and many a long year to come—the tradition of
genuine warm-hearted courteous Irish hospitality, which our forefathers
have handed down to us and which we in turn must hand down to our
descendants, is still alive among us."

A hearty murmur of assent ran round the table. It shot through
Gabriel's mind that Miss Ivors was not there and that she gone away
discourteously: and he said with confidence in himself:

"Ladies and Gentlemen,

"A new generation is growing up in our midst, a generation actuated
by new ideas and new principles. It is serious and enthusiastic for these
new ideas and its enthusiasm, even when it is misdirected, is, I believe,
in the main sincere. But we are living in a sceptical and, if I may use the
phrase, a thought-tormented age: and sometimes I fear that this new

generation, educated or hypereducated as it is, will lack those qualities of humanity, of hospitality, of kindly humour which belonged to an older day. Listening tonight to the names of all those great singers of the past it seemed to me, I must confess, that we were living in a less spacious age. Those days might, without exaggeration, be called spacious days: and if they are gone beyond recall let us hope, at least, that in gatherings such as this we shall still speak of them with pride and affection, still cherish in our hearts the memory of those dead and gone great ones whose fame the world will not willingly let die."

"Hear, hear!" said Mr. Browne loudly.

"But yet," continued Gabriel, his voice falling into a softer inflection, "there are always in gatherings such as this sadder thoughts that will recur to our minds: thoughts of the past, of youth, of changes, of absent faces that we miss here tonight. Our path through life is strewn with many such sad memories: and were we to brood upon them always we could not find the heart to go on bravely with our work among the living. We have all of us living duties and living affections which claim, and rightly claim, our strenuous endeavours.

"Therefore, I will not linger on the past. I will not let any gloomy moralising intrude upon us here tonight. Here we are gathered together for a brief moment from the bustle and rush of our everyday routine. We are met here as friends, in the spirit of good-fellowship, as colleagues, also to a certain extent, in the true spirit of *camaraderie,* and as the guests of—what shall I call them?—the Three Graces of the Dublin musical world."

The table burst into applause and laughter at this allusion. Aunt Julia vainly asked each of her neighbours in turn to tell her what Gabriel had said.

"He says we are the Three Graces, Aunt Julia," said Mary Jane.

Aunt Julia did not understand but she looked up, smiling, at Gabriel, who continued in the same vein:

"Ladies and Gentlemen,

"I will not attempt to play tonight the part that Paris played on another occasion. I will not attempt to choose between them. The Task would be an invidious one and one beyond my poor powers. For when I view them in turn, whether it be our chief hostess herself, whose good heart, whose too good heart, has become a byword with all who know her, or her sister, who seems to be gifted with perennial youth and whose singing must have been a surprise and a revelation to us all tonight, or, last but not least, when I consider our youngest hostess, talented, cheerful, hard-working and the best of nieces, I confess, Ladies and Gentlemen, that I do not know to which of them I should award the prize."

Gabriel glanced down at his aunts and, seeing the large smile on Aunt Julia's face and the tears which had risen to Aunt Kate's eyes, hastened to his close. He raised his glass of port gallantly, while every member of the company fingered a glass expectantly, and said loudly:

"Let us toast them all three together. Let us drink to their health, wealth, long life, happiness and prosperity and may they long continue to hold the proud and self-won position which they hold in their profession and the position of honour and affection which they hold in our hearts."

All the guests stood up, glass in hand, and turning towards the three seated ladies, sang in unison, with Mr. Browne as leader:

> For they are jolly gay fellows,
> For they are jolly gay fellows,
> For they are jolly gay fellows,
> Which nobody can deny.

Aunt Kate was making frank use of her handkerchief and even Aunt Julia seemed moved. Freddy Malins beat time with his pudding-fork and the singers turned towards one another, as if in melodious conference, while they sang with emphasis:

> Unless he tells a lie,
> Unless he tells a lie,

Then, turning once more towards their hostesses, they sang:

> For they are jolly gay fellows,
> For they are jolly gay fellows,
> For they are jolly gay fellows,
> Which nobody can deny.

The acclamation which followed was taken up beyond the door of the supper-room by many of the other guests and renewed time after time, Freddy Malins acting as officer with his fork on high.

. . . .

The piercing morning air came into the hall where they were standing so that Aunt Kate said:

"Close the door, somebody. Mrs. Malins will get her death of cold."

"Browne is out there, Aunt Kate," said Mary Jane.

"Browne is everywhere," said Aunt Kate, lowering her voice.

Mary Jane laughed at her tone.

"Really," she said archly, "he is very attentive."

"He has been laid on here like the gas," said Aunt Kate in the same tone, "all during the Christmas."

She laughed herself this time good-humouredly and then added quickly:

"But tell him to come in, Mary Jane, and close the door. I hope to goodness he didn't hear me."

At that moment the hall-door was opened and Mr. Browne came in from the doorstep, laughing as if his heart would break. He was dressed in a long green overcoat with mock astrakhan cuffs and collar and wore on his head an oval fur cap. He pointed down the snow-covered quay from where the sound of shrill prolonged whistling was borne in.

"Teddy will have all the cabs in Dublin out," he said.

Gabriel advanced from the little pantry behind the office, struggling into his overcoat and, looking round the hall, said:

"Gretta not down yet?"

"She's getting on her things, Gabriel," said Aunt Kate.

"Who's playing up there?" asked Gabriel.

"Nobody. They're all gone."

"O no, Aunt Kate," said Mary Jane. "Bartell D'Arcy and Miss O'Callaghan aren't gone yet."

"Someone is fooling at the piano anyhow," said Gabriel.

Mary Jane glanced at Gabriel and Mr. Browne and said with a shiver:

"It makes me feel cold to look at you two gentlemen muffled up like that. I wouldn't like to face your journey home at this hour."

"I'd like nothing better this minute," said Mr. Browne stoutly, "than a rattling fine walk in the country or a fast drive with a good spanking goer between the shafts."

"We used to have a very good horse and trap at home," said Aunt Julia sadly.

"The never-to-be-forgotten Johnny," said Mary Jane, laughing.

Aunt Kate and Gabriel laughed too.

"Why, what was wonderful about Johnny?" asked Mr. Browne.

"The late lamented Patrick Morkan, our grandfather, that is," explained Gabriel, "commonly known in his later years as the old gentleman, was a glue-boiler."

"O, now, Gabriel," said Aunt Kate, laughing, "he had a starch mill."

"Well, glue or starch," said Gabriel, "the old gentleman had a horse by the name of Johnny. And Johnny used to work in the old gentleman's mill, walking round and round in order to drive the mill. That was all very well; but now comes the tragic part about Johnny. One fine day the old gentleman thought he'd like to drive out with the quality to a military review in the park."

"The Lord have mercy on his soul," said Aunt Kate compassionately.

"Amen," said Gabriel. "So the old gentleman, as I said, harnessed Johnny and put on his very best tall hat and his very best stock collar and drove out in grand style from his ancestral mansion somewhere near Back Lane, I think."

Everyone laughed, even Mrs. Malins, at Gabriel's manner and Aunt Kate said:

"O, now, Gabriel, he didn't live in Back Lane, really. Only the mill was there."

"Out from the mansion of his forefathers," continued Gabriel, "he drove with Johnny. And everything went on beautifully until Johnny came in sight of King Billy's statue: and whether he fell in love with the horse King Billy sits on or whether he thought he was back again in the mill, anyhow he began to walk round the statue."

Gabriel paced in a circle round the hall in his goloshes amid the laughter of the others.

"Round and round he went," said Gabriel, "and the old gentleman, who was a very pompous old gentleman, was highly indignant. 'Go on, sir! What do you mean, sir? Johnny! Johnny! Most extraordinary conduct! Can't understand the horse!' "

The peal of laughter which followed Gabriel's imitation of the incident was interrupted by a resounding knock at the hall door. Mary Jane ran to open it and let in Freddy Malins. Freddy Malins, with his hat well back on his head and his shoulders humped with cold, was puffing and steaming after his exertions.

"I could only get one cab," he said.

"O, we'll find another along the quay," said Gabriel.

"Yes," said Aunt Kate. "Better not keep Mrs. Malins standing in the draught."

Mrs. Malins was helped down the front steps by her son and Mr. Browne and, after many manoeuvres, hoisted into the cab. Freddy Malins clambered in after her and spent a long time settling her on the seat, Mr. Browne helping him with advice. At last she was settled comfortably and Freddy Malins invited Mr. Browne into the cab. There was a good deal of confused talk, and then Mr. Browne got into the cab. The cabman settled his rug over his knees, and bent down for the address. The confusion grew greater and the cabman was directed differently by Freddy Malins and Mr. Browne, each of whom had his head out through a window of the cab. The difficulty was to know where to drop Mr. Browne along the route, and Aunt Kate, Aunt Julia and Mary Jane helped the discussion from the doorstep with cross-directions and contradictions and abundance of laughter. As for Freddy Malins he was speechless with laughter. He popped his head in and out of the window every moment to the great danger of his hat, and told his mother how the discussion was progressing, till at last Mr. Browne shouted to the bewildered cabman above the din of everybody's laughter:

"Do you know Trinity College?"

"Yes, sir," said the cabman.

"Well, drive bang up against Trinity College gates," said Mr. Browne, "and then we'll tell you where to go. You understand now?"

"Yes, sir," said the cabman.

"Make like a bird for Trinity College."

"Right, sir," said the cabman.

The horse was whipped up and the cab rattled off along the quay amid a chorus of laughter and adieus.

Gabriel had not gone to the door with the others. He was in a dark part of the hall gazing up the staircase. A woman was standing near the top of the first flight, in the shadow also. He could not see her face but he could see the terra-cotta and salmon-pink panels of her skirt which the shadow made appear black and white. It was his wife. She was leaning on the banisters, listening to something. Gabriel was surprised at her stillness and strained his ear to listen also. But he could hear little save the noise of laughter and dispute on the front steps, a few chords struck on the piano and a few notes of a man's voice singing.

He stood still in the gloom of the hall, trying to catch the air that the voice was singing and gazing up at his wife. There was grace and mystery in her attitude as if she were a symbol of something. He asked himself what is a woman standing on the stairs in the shadow, listening to distant music, a symbol of. If he were a painter he would paint her in that attitude. Her blue felt hat would show off the bronze of her hair against the darkness and the dark panels of her skirt would show off the light ones. *Distant Music* he would call the picture if he were a painter.

The hall-door was closed; and Aunt Kate, Aunt Julia and Mary Jane came down the hall, still laughing.

"Well, isn't Freddy terrible?" said Mary Jane. "He's really terrible."

Gabriel said nothing but pointed up the stairs towards where his wife was standing. Now that the hall-door was closed the voice and the piano could be heard more clearly. Gabriel held up his hand for them to be silent. The song seemed to be in the old Irish tonality and the singer seemed uncertain both of his words and of his voice. The voice, made plaintive by distance and by the singer's hoarseness, faintly illuminated the cadence of the air with words expressing grief:

> O, the rain falls on my heavy locks
> And the dew wets my skin,
> My babe lies cold . . .

"O," exclaimed Mary Jane. "It's Bartell D'Arcy singing and he wouldn't sing all the night. O, I'll get him to sing a song before he goes."

"O, do, Mary Jane," said Aunt Kate.

Mary Jane brushed past the others and ran to the staircase, but before she reached it the singing stopped and the piano was closed abruptly.

"O, what a pity!" she cried. "Is he coming down, Gretta?"

Gabriel heard his wife answer yes and saw her come down towards them. A few steps behind her were Mr. Bartell D'Arcy and Miss O'Callaghan.

"O, Mr. D'Arcy," cried Mary Jane, "it's downright mean of you to break off like that when we were all in raptures listening to you."

"I have been at him all the evening," said Miss O'Callaghan, "and

Mrs. Conroy, too, and he told us he had a dreadful cold and couldn't sing."

"O, Mr. D'Arcy," said Aunt Kate, "now that was a great fib to tell."

"Can't you see that I'm as hoarse as a crow?" said Mr. D'Arcy roughly.

He went into the pantry hastily and put on his overcoat. The others, taken aback by his rude speech, could find nothing to say. Aunt Kate wrinkled her brows and made signs to the others to drop the subject. Mr. D'Arcy stood swathing his neck carefully and frowning.

"It's the weather," said Aunt Julia, after a pause.

"Yes, everybody has colds," said Aunt Kate readily, "everybody."

"They say," said Mary Jane, "we haven't had snow like it for thirty years; and I read this morning in the newspapers that the snow is general all over Ireland."

"I love the look of snow," said Aunt Julia sadly.

"So do I," said Miss O'Callaghan. "I think Christmas is never really Christmas unless we have the snow on the ground."

"But poor Mr. D'Arcy doesn't like the snow," said Aunt Kate, smiling.

Mr. D'Arcy came from the pantry, fully swathed and buttoned, and in a repentant tone told them the history of his cold. Everyone gave him advice and said it was a great pity and urged him to be very careful of his throat in the night air. Gabriel watched his wife, who did not join in the conversation. She was standing right under the dusty fanlight and the flame of the gas lit up the rich bronze of her hair, which he had seen her drying at the fire a few days before. She was in the same attitude and seemed unaware of the talk about her. At last she turned towards them and Gabriel saw that there was colour on her cheeks and that her eyes were shining. A sudden tide of joy went leaping out of his heart.

"Mr. D'Arcy," she said, "what is the name of that song you were singing?"

"It's called The Lass of Aughrim," said Mr. D'Arcy, "but I couldn't remember it properly. Why? Do you know it?"

"The Lass of Aughrim," she repeated. "I couldn't think of the name."

"It's a very nice air," said Mary Jane. "I'm sorry you were not in voice tonight."

"Now, Mary Jane," said Aunt Kate, "don't annoy Mr. D'Arcy. I won't have him annoyed."

Seeing that all were ready to start she shepherded them to the door, where good-night was said:

"Well, good-night, Aunt Kate, and thanks for the pleasant evening."

"Good-night, Gabriel. Good-night, Gretta!"

"Good-night, Aunt Kate, and thanks ever so much. Good-night, Aunt Julia."

"O, good-night, Gretta. I didn't see you."

"Good-night, Mr. D'Arcy. Good-night, Miss O'Callaghan."

"Good-night, Miss Morkan."

"Good-night, again."

"Good-night, all. Safe home."

"Good-night. Good night."

The morning was still dark. A dull, yellow light brooded over the houses and the river; and the sky seemed to be descending. It was slushy underfoot; and only streaks and patches of snow lay on the roofs, on the parapets of the quay and on the area railings. The lamps were still burning redly in the murky air and, across the river, the palace of the Four Courts stood out menacingly against the heavy sky.

She was walking on before him with Mr. Bartell D'Arcy, her shoes in a brown parcel tucked under one arm and her hands holding her skirt up from the slush. She had no longer any grace of attitude, but Gabriel's eyes were still bright with happiness. The blood went bounding along his veins; and the thoughts went rioting through his brain, proud, joyful, tender, valorous.

She was walking on before him so lightly and so erect that he longed to run after her noiselessly, catch her by the shoulders and say something foolish and affectionate into her ear. She seemed to him so frail that he longed to defend her against something and then to be alone with her. Moments of their secret life together burst like stars upon his memory. A heliotrope envelope was lying beside his breakfast cup and he was caressing it with his hand. Birds were twittering in the ivy and the sunny web of the curtain was shimmering along the floor: he could not eat for happiness. They were standing on the crowded platform and he was placing a ticket inside the warm palm of her glove. He was standing with her in the cold, looking in through a grated window at a man making bottles in a roaring furnace. It was very cold. Her face, fragrant in the cold air, was quite close to his; and suddenly he called out to the man at the furnace:

"Is the fire hot, sir?"

But the man could not hear with the noise of the furnace. It was just as well. He might have answered rudely.

A wave of yet more tender joy escaped from his heart and went coursing in warm flood along his arteries. Like the tender fire of stars moments of their life together, that no one knew of or would ever know of, broke upon and illumined his memory. He longed to recall to her those moments, to make her forget the years of their dull existence together and remember only their moments of ecstasy. For the years, he felt, had not quenched his soul or hers. Their children, his writing, her household cares had not quenched all their soul's tender fire. In one letter he had written to her then he had said: "Why is it that words like these seem to me so dull and cold? Is it because there is no word tender enough to be your name?"

Like distant music these words that he had written years before were borne towards him from the past. He longed to be alone with her. When the others had gone away, when he and she were in the room in the hotel, then they would be alone together. He would call her softly:

"Gretta!"

Perhaps she would not hear at once: she would be undressing. Then something in his voice would strike her. She would turn and look at him. . . .

At the corner of Winetavern Street they met a cab. He was glad of its rattling noise as it saved him from conversation. She was looking out of the window and seemed tired. The others spoke only a few words, pointing out some building or street. The horse galloped along wearily under the murky morning sky, dragging his old rattling box after his heels, and Gabriel was again in a cab with her, galloping to catch the boat, galloping to their honeymoon.

As the cab drove across O'Connell Bridge Miss O'Callaghan said:

"They say you never cross O'Connell Bridge without seeing a white horse."

"I see a white man this time," said Gabriel.

"Where?" asked Mr. Bartell D'Arcy.

Gabriel pointed to the statue, on which lay patches of snow. Then he nodded familiarly to it and waved his hand.

"Good-night, Dan," he said gaily.

When the cab drew up before the hotel, Gabriel jumped out and, in spite of Mr. Bartell D'Arcy's protest, paid the driver. He gave the man a shilling over his fare. The man saluted and said:

"A prosperous New Year to you, sir."

"The same to you," said Gabriel cordially.

She leaned for a moment on his arm in getting out of the cab and while standing at the curbstone, bidding the others good-night. She leaned lightly on his arm, as lightly as when she had danced with him a few hours before. He had felt proud and happy then, happy that she was his, proud of her grace and wifely carriage. But now, after the kindling again of so many memories, the first touch of her body, musical and strange and perfumed, sent through him a keen pang of lust. Under cover of her silence he pressed her arm closely to his side; and, as they stood at the hotel door, he felt that they had escaped from their lives and duties, escaped from home and friends and run away together with wild and radiant hearts to a new adventure.

An old man was dozing in a great hooded chair in the hall. He lit a candle in the office and went before them to the stairs. They followed him in silence, their feet falling in soft thuds on the thickly carpeted stairs. She mounted the stairs behind the porter, her head bowed in the ascent, her frail shoulders curved as with a burden, her skirt girt tightly about her. He could have flung his arms about her hips and held her still, for his arms were trembling with desire to seize her and only the stress of his nails against the palms of his hands held the wild impulse of his body in check. The porter halted on the stairs to settle his guttering candle. They halted, too, on the steps below him. In the silence Gabriel could hear the falling of the molten wax into the tray and the thumping of his own heart against his ribs.

The porter led them along a corridor and opened a door. Then he set his unstable candle down on a toilet-table and asked at what hour they were to be called in the morning.

"Eight," said Gabriel.

The porter pointed to the tap of the electric-light and began a muttered apology, but Gabriel cut him short.

"We don't want any light. We have light enough from the street. And I say," he added, pointing to the candle, "you might remove that handsome article, like a good man."

The porter took up his candle again, but slowly, for he was surprised by such a novel idea. Then he mumbled good-night and went out. Gabriel shot the lock to.

A ghastly light from the street lamp lay in a long shaft from one window to the door. Gabriel threw his overcoat and hat on a couch and crossed the room towards the window. He looked down into the street in order that his emotion might calm a little. Then he turned and leaned against a chest of drawers with his back to the light. She had taken off her hat and cloak and was standing before a large swinging mirror, unhooking her waist. Gabriel paused for a few moments, watching her, and then said:

"Gretta!"

She turned away from the mirror slowly and walked along the shaft of light towards him. Her face looked so serious and weary that the words would not pass Gabriel's lips. No, it was not the moment yet.

"You look tired," he said.

"I am a little," she answered.

"You don't feel ill or weak?"

"No, tired: that's all."

She went on to the window and stood there, looking out. Gabriel waited again and then, fearing that diffidence was about to conquer him, he said abruptly:

"By the way, Gretta!"

"What is it?"

"You know that poor fellow Malins?" he said quickly.

"Yes, What about him?"

"Well, poor fellow, he's a decent sort of chap, after all," continued Gabriel in a false voice. "He gave me back that sovereign I lent him, and I didn't expect it, really. It's a pity he wouldn't keep away from that Browne, because he's not a bad fellow, really."

He was trembling now with annoyance. Why did she seem so abstracted? He did not know how he could begin. Was she annoyed, too, about something? If she would only turn to him or come to him of her own accord! To take her as she was would be brutal. No, he must see some ardour in her eyes first. He longed to be master of her strange mood.

"When did you lend him the pound?" she asked, after a pause.

Gabriel strove to restrain himself from breaking out into brutal language about the sottish Malins and his pound. He longed to cry to her from his soul, to crush her body against his, to overmaster her. But he said:

"O, at Christmas, when he opened that little Christmas-card shop in Henry Street."

He was in such a fever of rage and desire that he did not hear her come from the window. She stood before him for an instant, looking at him strangely. Then, suddenly raising herself on tiptoe and resting her hands lightly on his shoulders, she kissed him.

"You are a very generous person, Gabriel," she said.

Gabriel, trembling with delight at her sudden kiss and at the quaintness of her phrase, put his hands on her hair and began smoothing it back, scarcely touching it with his fingers. The washing had made it fine and brilliant. His heart was brimming over with happiness. Just when he was wishing for it she had come to him of her own accord. Perhaps her thoughts had been running with his. Perhaps she had felt the impetuous desire that was in him, and then the yielding mood had come upon her. Now that she had fallen to him so easily, he wondered why he had been so diffident.

He stood, holding her head between his hands. Then, slipping one arm swiftly about her body and drawing her towards him, he said softly:

"Gretta, dear, what are you thinking about?"

She did not answer or yield wholly to his arm. He said again, softly:

"Tell me what it is, Gretta. I think I know what is the matter. Do I know?"

She did not answer at once. Then she said in an outburst of tears:

"O, I am thinking about that song, The Lass of Aughrim."

She broke loose from him and ran to the bed and, throwing her arms across the bed-rail, hid her face. Gabriel stood stock-still for a moment in astonishment and then followed her. As he passed in the way of the cheval-glass he caught sight of himself in full length, his broad, well-filled shirtfront, the face whose expression always puzzled. him when he saw it in a mirror, and his glimmering gilt-rimmed eye-glasses. He halted a few paces from her and said:

"What about the song? Why does that make you cry?"

She raised her head from her arms and dried her eyes with the back of her hand like a child. A kinder note than he had intended went into his voice.

"Why, Gretta?" he asked.

"I am thinking about a person long ago who used to sing that song."

"And who was the person long ago?" asked Gabriel, smiling.

"It was a person I used to know in Galway when I was living with my grandmother," she said.

The smile passed away from Gabriel's face. A dull anger began to gather again at the back of his mind and the dull fires of his lust began to glow angrily in his veins.

"Someone you were in love with?" he asked ironically.

"It was a young boy I used to know," she answered, "named Michael Furey. He used to sing that song, *The Lass of Aughrim*. He was very delicate."

Gabriel was silent. He did not wish her to think that he was interested in this delicate boy.

"I can see him so plainly," she said, after a moment. "Such eyes as he had: big, dark eyes! And such an expression in them—an expression!"

"O, then, you are in love with him?" said Gabriel.

"I used to go out walking with him," she said, "when I was in Galway."

A thought flew across Gabriel's mind.

"Perhaps that was why you wanted to go to Galway with that Ivors girl?" he said coldly.

She looked at him and asked in surprise:

"What for?"

Her eyes made Gabriel feel awkward. He shrugged his shoulders and said:

"How do I know? To see him, perhaps."

She looked away from him along the shaft of light towards the window in silence.

"He is dead," she said at length. "He died when he was only seventeen. Isn't it a terrible thing to die so young as that?"

"What was he?" asked Gabriel, still ironically.

"He was in the gasworks," she said.

Gabriel felt humiliated by the failure of his irony and by the evocation of this figure from the dead, a boy in the gasworks. While he had been full of memories of their secret life together, full of tenderness and joy and desire, she had been comparing him in her mind with another. A shameful consciousness of his own person assailed him. He saw himself as a ludicrous figure, acting as a pennyboy for his aunts, a nervous, well-meaning sentimentalist, orating to vulgarians and idealising his own clownish lusts, the pitiable fatuous fellow he had caught a glimpse of in the mirror. Instinctively he turned his back more to the light lest she might see the shame that burned upon his forehead.

He tried to keep up his tone of cold interrogation, but his voice when he spoke was humble and indifferent.

"I suppose you were in love with this Michael Furey, Gretta," he said.

"I was great with him at that time," she said.

Her voice was veiled and sad. Gabriel, feeling now how vain it would be to try to lead her whither he had purposed, caressed one of her hands and said, also sadly:

"And what did he die of so young, Gretta? Consumption, was it?"

"I think he died for me," she answered.

A vague terror seized Gabriel at this answer, as if, at that hour when he had hoped to triumph, some impalpable and vindictive being was coming against him, gathering forces against him in its vague world. But he shook himself free of it with an effort of reason and continued to caress her hand. He did not question her again, for he felt that she would tell him of herself. Her hand was warm and moist: it did not respond to his touch, but he continued to caress it just as he had caressed her first letter to him that spring morning.

"It was in the winter," she said, "about the beginning of the winter when I was going to leave my grandmother's and come up here to the convent. And he was ill at the time in his lodgings in Galway and wouldn't be let out, and his people in Oughterard were written to. He was in decline, they said, or something like that. I never knew rightly."

She paused for a moment and sighed.

"Poor fellow," she said. "He was very fond of me and he was such a gentle boy. We used to go out together, walking, you know, Gabriel, like the way they do in the country. He was going to study singing only for his health. He had a very good voice, poor Michael Furey."

"Well; and then?" asked Gabriel.

"And then when it came to the time for me to leave Galway and come up to the convent he was much worse and I wouldn't be let see him so I wrote him a letter saying I was going up to Dublin and would be back in the summer, and hoping he would be better then."

She paused for a moment to get her voice under control, and then went on:

"Then the night before I left, I was in my grandmother's house in Nuns' Island, packing up, and I heard gravel thrown up against the window. The window was so wet I couldn't see, so I ran downstairs as I was and slipped out the back into the garden and there was the poor fellow at the end of the garden, shivering."

"And did you not tell him to go back?" asked Gabriel.

"I implored of him to go home at once and told him he would get his death in the rain. But he said he did not want to live. I can see his eyes as well as well! He was standing at the end of the wall where there was a tree."

"And did he go home?" asked Gabriel.

"Yes, he went home. And when I was only a week in the convent he died and he was buried in Oughterard, where his people came from. O, the day I heard that, that he was dead!"

She stopped, choking with sobs, and, overcome by emotion, flung herself face downward on the bed, sobbing in the quilt. Gabriel held her hand for a moment longer, irresolutely, and then, shy of intruding on her grief, let it fall gently and walked quietly to the window.

She was fast asleep.

Gabriel, leaning on his elbow, looked for a few moments unresentfully on her tangled hair and half-open mouth, listening to her deep-drawn breath. So she had had that romance in her life: a man had died for her sake. It hardly pained him now to think how poor a part he, her husband, had played in her life. He watched her while she slept, as though he and she had never lived together as man and wife. His curious eyes rested long upon her face and on her hair: and, as he thought of what she must have been then, in that time of her first girlish beauty, a strange, friendly pity for her entered his soul. He did not like to say even to himself that her face was no longer beautiful, but he knew that it was no longer the face for which Michael Furey had braved death.

Perhaps she had not told him all the story. His eyes moved to the chair over which she had thrown some of her clothes. A petticoat string dangled to the floor. One boot stood upright, its limp upper fallen down: the fellow of it lay upon its side. He wondered at his riot of emotions of an hour before. From what had it proceeded? From his aunt's supper, from his own foolish speech, from the wine and dancing, the merry-making when saying good-night in the hall, the pleasure of the walk along the river in the snow. Poor Aunt Julia! She, too, would soon be a shade with the shade of Patrick Morkan and his horse. He had caught that haggard look upon her face for a moment when she was singing *Arrayed for the Bridal*. Soon, perhaps, he would be sitting in that same drawing-room, dressed in black, his silk hat on his knees. The blinds would be drawn down and Aunt Kate would be sitting beside him, crying and blowing her nose and telling him how Julia had died. He would cast about in his mind for some words that might console her, and would find only lame and useless ones. Yes, yes: that would happen very soon.

The air of the room chilled his shoulders. He stretched himself cautiously along under the sheets and lay down beside his wife. One by one, they were all becoming shades. Better pass boldly into that other world, in the full glory of some passion, than fade and wither dismally with age. He thought of how she who lay beside him had locked in her heart for so many years that image of her lover's eyes when he had told her that he did not wish to live.

Generous tears filled Gabriel's eyes. He had never felt like that himself towards any woman, but he knew that such a feeling must be love. The tears gathered more thickly in his eyes and in the partial darkness he imagined he saw the form of a young man standing under a dripping tree. Other forms were near. His soul had approached that region where dwell the vast hosts of the dead. He was conscious of, but could not apprehend, their wayward and flickering existence. His own identity was fading out into a grey impalpable world: the solid world itself, which these dead had one time reared and lived in, was dissolving and dwindling.

A few light taps upon the pane made him turn to the window. It had begun to snow again. He watched sleepily the flakes, silver and dark, falling obliquely against the lamplight. The time had come for him to set out on his journey westward. Yes, the newspapers were right: snow was general all over Ireland. It was falling on every part of the dark central plain, on the treeless hills, falling softly upon the Bog of Allen and, farther westward, softly falling into the dark mutinous Shannon waves. It was falling, too, upon every part of the lonely churchyard on the hill where Michael Furey lay buried. It lay thickly drifted on the crooked crosses and headstones, on the spears of the little gate, on the barren thorns. His soul swooned slowly as he heard the snow falling faintly through the universe and faintly falling, like the descent of their last end, upon all the living and the dead.

PART TWO

✵

✵

THE STORY IN CONTEXT

A CHRONOLOGY OF THE LIFE OF JAMES JOYCE*

Richard Ellmann

1882	On 2 February James Joyce was born at 41 Brighton Square, Rathgar, Dublin. He was the eldest son of John Stanislaus Joyce, rate collector, and Mary Jane Joyce (nee Murray). Of the fifteen children in the family, only ten survived infancy; among these Joyce had the closest relationship with his brother Stanislaus, born 17 December 1885.
1888	The Joyce family had moved to Bray, and in September Joyce was sent to Clongowes Wood College (Jesuit), where he remained until June 1891, returning home only for holidays.
1891	Late in 1891 Joyce, fired by the death of Parnell on 6 October, wrote a verse broadside, his first printed work, with the title of *Et Tu, Healy*. It celebrated the dead hero and attacked his chief political enemy. No copy survives.
1893–98	Joyce, withdrawn from Clongowes when the family fortunes began to decline, was sent to Belvedere College, also a Jesuit school, from April 1893. He made a brilliant record, winning several prizes in the intermediate examinations.
1899–1902	Joyce's career at University College, Dublin, was marked by his break with his Catholic background and his emergence as a writer. In May 1899, he refused to join a protest against the heresy of Yeats's *Countess Cathleen*. On 20 January 1900 he read a paper on 'Drama and Life' before the Literary and Historical Society; his essay on 'Ibsen's New Drama' (*When We Dead Awaken*) was published in the *Fortnightly Review* for April 1900; a pamphlet, 'The Day of the Rabblement', attacking the parochialism of the Irish Literary Theatre, was written on 15 October 1901; an essay on 'James Clarence Mangan' was published in May 1902. During this period, also, he wrote a play entitled *A Brilliant Career* and translated two plays of Hauptmann.

* From *Letters of James Joyce* edited by Stuart Gilbert. Copyright © 1957 by The Viking Press, Inc. Reprinted by permission of The Viking Press. Inc. and The Society of Authors.

After receiving his degree on 31 October 1902, Joyce considered attending medical school in Dublin, but decided to study in Paris instead. He planned to be both doctor and writer. Leaving Dublin in late November, he stopped briefly in London to see W. B. Yeats, Arthur Symons, and various editors, then proceeded to Paris. There he quickly abandoned his medical studies, but lived the life of a Bohemian student, fascinated by the scene and usually its hungriest observer. Twenty-three book reviews by him appeared in a Dublin newspaper from 11 December 1902 to 19 November 1903.

1903   In April his mother's last illness began; on receipt of an urgent telegram from his father, Joyce returned to Dublin. Mary Jane Joyce died on 13 August.

1904   7 January is the date of the first draft of *Stephen Hero,* a later version of which was published (posthumously) in 1944.

About March Joyce obtained a position as teacher at the Clifton School, Dalkley, where he remained until the end of June. On 16 May he sang at the Feis Ceoil, a music festival, but failed to win because he could not read music at sight. About 10 June he met Nora Barnacle, and shortly thereafter, perhaps on 16 June (the day he later chose as the date for *Ulysses*), fell in love with her. Opposed to marriage and unable to live openly with her in Dublin, he decided to return to the Continent. Before leaving he wrote the satirical broadside, 'The Holy Office', distributed not long after his departure on 8 October.

Upon arriving with Nora in Zurich he found that his expected position as teacher at the Berlitz School was not available, and proceeded to Pola (now in Yugoslavia) to teach English at the Berlitz School there.

During 1904 his first published poems and stories appeared.

1905   In March Joyce was transferred to the Berlitz School in Trieste.

On 27 July his son Giorgio was born.

In September his difficulties with publishers began with the rejection by Grant Richards of *Chamber Music.*

In October Stanislaus Joyce, at his brother's urging, came to live in Trieste.

At the end of November the submission of the manuscript of *Dubliners* to Grant Richards started a contentious correspondence over the book.

1906   In July Joyce, bored with Trieste, took his wife and son to Rome, where a position in a bank awaited him.

1907   On 17 January 1907 he contracted with Elkin Mathews for the publication of *Chamber Music*.

   In March, Rome having proved unsatisfactory, Joyce returned to Trieste, where after a brief spell of teaching at the Berlitz School he found private lessons more profitable.

   Early in May *Chamber Music* was published.

   On 26 July, St. Anne's Day his daughter Lucia Anna was born.

1909   On 1 August Joyce returned to Ireland for a visit. At the beginning of September he signed a contract for the publication of *Dubliners* by Maunsel & Co. in Dublin. On 9 September he returned to Trieste, and interested some businessmen there in starting up cinemas in Ireland. With their backing he returned to Dublin on 21 October and opened the Cinematograph Volta on 20 December.

1910   Unwilling to remain as manager, Joyce returned to Trieste in January, and the Volta was soon after sold. In July Maunsel & Co., suddenly fearful because of the candour of *Dubliners,* postponed publication of the book.

1912   From July to September Joyce made his last trip to Ireland, going to Galway as well as Dublin. He was unable to persuade Maunsel & Co. to publish *Dubliners* and the printer broke up the type. Joyce's impressions of Dublin was summarized in the broadside, 'Gas from a Burner', written on his return journey.

1913   Through Yeats's intercession Joyce was brought into communication with Ezra Pound, who interested Miss Dora Marsden, the editor of the *Egoist,* in his work.

1914   A lucky year: in January Grant Richards agreed to publish *Dubliners*, and did so on 15 June. From 2 February 1914 to 1 September 1915 *A Portrait of the Artist as a Young Man* was published (thanks to Miss Dora Marsden and subsequently to Miss Weaver, who was to become his patron) in the *Egoist* (London) in serial form. In March Joyce began work on *Ulysses*, but put it aside for a time to write *Exiles*, finished in 1915.

1915   Although his brother was interned because of the war at the beginning of 1915, Joyce was left undisturbed in Trieste by the Austrian authorities. At the end of June he was permitted to depart for Switzerland on his word of honour to remain neutral. In August, through the intercession of Pound, Edmund Gosse, and Yeats, he received a gift of money from the Royal Literary Fund.

1916   In September he received a grant from the British Treasury Fund.

1917

On 29 December the *Portrait* was published in New York. On 12 February the *Portrait* was published in London. Later this year Joyce received a first gift from Miss Weaver.

During this year Joyce's eye troubles grew worse and made necessary his first eye operation late in the summer. On 12 October he went to Locarno to recover in the milder climate.

1918

In January Joyce returned to Zurich. Here Mrs Harold McCormick gave him a monthly stipend to enable him to write. Temporarily in funds, he organized, with Claud W. Sykes, the English Players, whose first production, Wilde's *Importance of Being Earnest,* took place on 29 April. A quarrel with the leading actor over salary brought about two inconclusive lawsuits, the first in October 1918, the second in February 1919.

In March the *Little Review* (New York) began to publish *Ulysses* in serial form, completing half the book by the end of 1920.

On 25 May *Exiles* was published in England and the United States.

1919

Early in the autumn Mrs McCormick withdrew her subsidy, and in October Joyce returned with his family to Trieste. There he taught English at a commercial school and worked hard at *Ulysses.*

1920

In June Joyce went with his son to Desenzano, Italy, to meet Ezra Pound, who persuaded him to come to live in Paris so as to promote the publication of his work. The same month the Joyce family moved to Paris.

In October the Society for the Suppression of Vice lodged a complaint against the *Little Review* in New York for publishing certain passages of *Ulysses.*

1921

The final stages of preparing *Ulysses* for the public: in April Joyce agreed to have Sylvia Beach publish it in Paris. On 7 December Valery Larbaud, who had read the manuscript, delivered a eulogistic lecture on *Ulysses,* which, published in the *Nouvelle Revue Française* in April 1922, set the key for the critical reception.

1922

On 2 February, Joyce's birthday, *Ulysses* was published.

On 1 April Nora Joyce took the two children to Ireland to visit her mother, but was obliged to leave at once because of the Irish civil war. In May Joyce planned a trip to London but gave it up because of eye trouble. He went there, however, in August, returning to Paris in late September, then in mid-October went to Nice, intending to winter there. Because of pressure of affairs he returned to Paris.

1923   On 10 March Joyce wrote a first sketch for a character in *Finnegans Wake*.

From late June to mid-August, he and his family went to London, Bognor (on the Sussex coast), and London again.

1924   Another year of severe eye trouble.

In April 1924 the first fragment of *Finnegans Wake* was published in the *Transatlantic Review* (Paris).

From July to mid-August the Joyces were at St Malo and Quimper in Brittany: they returned to Paris at the beginning of September and late in the month went to London for about three weeks.

1925   In July the *Criterion* (London) published a second fragment from *Finnegans Wake*.

Late in July Joyce was at Fécamp; in August at Arcachon, returning to Paris early in September.

On 1 October the *Navire d'Argent* (Paris) published *Anna Livia Plurabelle*.

1926   From late July to September at Ostend and Brussels.

1927   During 1927 Joyce, in a fit of depression over *Finnegans Wake* and his friends' comments on it, considered abandoning the book.

On 2 February an international protest against the piracy of *Ulysses* in the United States was promulgated.

From April 1927 to May 1938 sections of *Finnegans Wake* were published in transition (Paris) by Eugene Jolas.

In April Joyce went to London to be guest of honour at a dinner of the P.E.N. Club. He spent May and June at The Hague and Amsterdam.

On 5 July *Pomes Penyeach* was published.

1928   In March Joyce went to Dieppe and Rouen; at the end of April he was in Toulon, returning in May. From July to mid-September he was at Salzburg.

On 20 October *Anna Livia Plurabelle* was published in book form. Mrs. Joyce had a serious but successful operation in November, after their return to Paris.

The French translation of *Ulysses* was published in February.

During July and August Joyce spent a few days in London, a month in Torquay, a few days in Bristol.

In August *Tales Told of Shem and Shaun* was published.

1930   In January Joyce began his efforts, which would last into 1934, to promote the career of John Sullivan, Irish-French tenor.

In May and June Dr. Alfred Vogt began a series of eye operations on Joyce in Zurich.

In June *Haveth Childers Everywhere* was published.

During July and August Joyce was in London, then for a few days in Oxford, and then in Llandudno (Wales). In September he was briefly at Étretat, where he was involved in a motor accident.

On 10 December Giorgio Joyce and Helen Kastor Fleischmann were married.

1931 In April Joyce spent a few days at Wiesbaden; at the end of the month he gave up his Paris flat, and in May went to London. He took a flat in Kensington and furnished it, intending to set up an English domicile. On 4 July he and Nora Joyce were married at a registry office in London 'for testamentary reasons'. In September they let their London flat and returned to Paris, where they took a furnished flat for the winter.

On 29 December Joyce's father, John Stanislaus Joyce, died in Dublin at the age of 82.

1932 On 15 February a grandson, Stephen James Joyce, was born.

In March Lucia Joyce suffered a mental breakdown, the first serious indication of her schizophrenia. The Joyces had planned to go to London in April, but her violent protests broke off the trip. From July to September they were at Zurich, and made a short visit to see Lucia at Feldkirch (Austria), where she was staying with Mrs Eugene Jolas. They then returned to Zurich and after the middle of September went on to Nice, where Lucia joined them.

During this year Paul Léon became Joyce's principal helper.

1933 In May the Joyces went to Zurich. They spent the summer at Evian (on the Lake of Geneva) to take the waters and be near Lucia who was in an institution in the neighbourhood.

On 6 December Judge John M. Woolsey issued his famous decision on *Ulysses*, ruling that it was not pornographic and making possible its American publication.

1934 In February *Ulysses* was published in New York.

During March Joyce went on a motor tour with friends to Grenoble, Zurich, and Monte Carlo. In April he went to consult Dr Vogt in Zurich.

In May 1934 Giorgio Joyce and his family went to the United States, where they remained until November 1935.

In June *The Mime of Mick Nick and the Maggies* was published.

At the end of July Joyce went to Spa, Belgium; in September he travelled to Zurich and Geneva, remaining in Zurich until the end of the year so as to be near Lucia.

1935 At the end of January Joyce returned to Paris from Zurich. In February Lucia went to London, and she spent March to July in Dublin, her mind showing increasing signs of strain. From August to December she stayed with Miss Weaver.

In September Joyce spent some days at Fontainebleau.

1936 On 26 July *A Chaucer A B C*, with initial letters by Lucia Joyce, was published as part of her father's frantic efforts to make her well.

During August and September the Joyces were in Denmark, and also visited Bonn en route.

In December *Collected Poems* was published.

1937 In August the Joyces were in Zurich, in September at Dieppe.

In October *Storiella as She Is Syung*, the last fragment of *Finnegans Wake* to appear separately in book form, was published.

1938 From August to September the Joyces were in Zurich and Lausanne.

1939 On 2 February Joyce exhibited a first bound copy of *Finnegans Wake*, although the book was not officially published in England and America until 4 May.

In July the Joyces were at Étretat, in August at Berne; when war was declared they were in Zurich. Returning to France they stayed at La Baule, to be near Lucia's *maison de santé*, from September to December. In December they went to St. Gérand-le-Puy, near Vichy.

1940 On 14 December the Joyces left St Gerand-le-Puy for Zurich, after elaborate negotiations for themselves and prolonged but unsuccessful efforts to enable Lucia, whose *permis de sortir* had expired meanwhile, to accompany them.

1941 Joyce died 13 January, at 2 a.m., in the Schwesterhaus vom Roten Kreuz in Zurich, as a result of a perforated ulcer.

THE BACKGROUNDS OF "THE DEAD"*

Richard Ellmann

The silent cock shall crow at last. The west shall shake the east awake.
Walk while ye have the night for morn, lightbreakfastbringer. . . .
—*Finnegans Wake* (473)

The stay in Rome had seemed purposeless, but during it Joyce became aware of the change in his attitude toward Ireland and so toward the world. He embodied his new perception in 'The Dead.' The story, which was the culmination of a long waiting history, began to take shape in Rome, but was not set down until he left the city. The pressure of hints, sudden insights, and old memories rose in his mind until, like King Midas's barber, he was compelled to speech.

Although the story dealt mainly with three generations of his family in Dublin, it drew also upon an incident in Galway in 1903. There Michael ('Sonny') Bodkin courted Nora Barnacle; but he contracted tuberculosis and had to be confined to bed. Shortly afterwards Nora resolved to go to Dublin, and Bodkin stole out of his sickroom, in spite of the rainy weather, to sing to her under an apple tree and bid her goodbye. In Dublin Nora soon learned that Bodkin was dead, and when she met Joyce she was first attracted to him, as she told a sister, because he resembled Sonny Bodkin.[1]

Joyce's habit of ferreting out details had made him conduct minute interrogations of Nora even before their departure from Dublin. He was disconcerted by the fact that young men before him had interested her. He did not much like to know that her heart was still moved, even in pity, by the recollection of the boy who had loved her. The notion of being in some sense in rivalry with a dead man buried in the little cemetery at Oughterard was one that came easily, and gallingly, to a man of Joyce's jealous disposition. It was one source of his complaint to his Aunt Josephine Murray that Nora persisted in regarding him as quite similar to other men she had known.[2]

* From *James Joyce* by Richard Ellmann. © 1959 by Richard Ellmann. Reprinted by permission of Oxford University Press, Inc. In the following excerpt page references apply to the Oxford University Press text.
[1] Letter to me from Mrs. Kathleen Barnacle Griffin.

A few months after expressing this annoyance, while Joyce and Nora Barnacle were living in Trieste in 1905, Joyce received another impulsion toward 'The Dead.' In a letter Stanislaus happened to mention attending a concert of Plunket Greene, the Irish baritone, which included one of Thomas Moore's *Irish Melodies* called 'O, Ye Dead!'[3] The song, a dialogue of living and dead, was eerie enough, but what impressed Stanislaus was that Greene rendered the second stanza, in which the dead answer the living, as if they were whimpering for the bodied existence they could no longer enjoy:

> It is true, it is true, we are shadows cold and wan;
> And the fair and the brave whom we loved on earth are gone;
> But still thus ev'n in death,
> So sweet the living breath
> Of the fields and the flow'rs in our youth we wandered o'er,
> That ere, condemn'd, we go
> To freeze, 'mid Hecla's snow,
> We would taste it awhile, and think we live once more!

James was interested and asked Stanislaus to send the words, which he learned to sing himself. His feelings about his wife's dead lover found a dramatic counterpart in the jealousy of the dead for the living in Moore's song: it would seem that the living and the dead are jealous of each other. Another aspect of the rivalry is suggested in *Ulysses*, where Stephen cries out to his mother's ghost, whose 'glazing eyes, staring out of death, to shake and bend my soul, . . . to strike me down,' he cannot put out of mind: 'No, mother. Let me be and let me live.'[4] That the dead do not stay buried is, in fact, a theme of Joyce from the beginning to the end of his work; Finnegan is not the only corpse to be resurrected.

In Rome the obtrusiveness of the dead affected what he thought of Dublin, the equally Catholic city he had abandoned, a city as prehensile of its ruins, visible and invisible. His head was filled with a sense of the too successful encroachment of the dead upon the living city; there was a disrupting parallel in the way that Dublin, buried behind him, was haunting his thoughts. In *Ulysses* the theme was to be reconstituted, in more horrid form, in the mind of Stephen, who sees corpses rising from their graves like vampires to deprive the living of joy. The bridebed, the childbed, and the bed of death are bound together, and death 'comes, pale vampire, through storm his eyes, his bat sails bloody-

---

[2] See p. 222.
[3] S. Joyce, 'The Background to "Dubliners," ' *Listener*, LI (March 25, 1954), 526–7.
[4] *Ulysses*, p. 12 (8).

ing the sea, mouth to her mouth's kiss.'[5] We can be at the same time in death as well as in life.*

By February 11, 1907, after six months in Rome, Joyce knew in general what story he must write. Some of his difficulty in beginning it was due, as he said himself, to the riot in Dublin over *The Playboy of the Western World*. Synge had followed the advice of Yeats that Joyce had rejected, to find his inspiration in the Irish folk, and had gone to the Aran Islands. This old issue finds small echoes in the story. The nationalistic Miss Ivors tries to persuade Gabriel to go to Aran (where Synge's *Riders to the Sea* is set), and when he refuses twits him for his lack of patriotic feeling. Though Gabriel thinks of defending the autonomy of art and its indifference to politics, he knows such a defense would be pretentious, and only musters up the remark that he is sick of his own country. But the issue is far from settled for him.

'The Dead' begins with a party and ends with a corpse, so entwining 'funferal' and 'funeral' as in the wake of Finnegan. That he began with a party was due, at least in part, to Joyce's feeling that the rest of the stories in *Dubliners* had not completed his picture of the city. In a letter of September 25, 1906, he had written his brother from Rome to say that some elements of Dublin had been left out of his stories: 'I have not reproduced its ingenuous insularity and its hospitality, the latter "virtue" so far as I can see does not exist elsewhere in Europe.' He allowed a little of this warmth to enter 'The Dead.' In his speech at the Christmas party Gabriel Conroy explicity commends Ireland for this very virtue of hospitality, though his expression of the idea is distinctly after-dinner: 'I feel more strongly with every recurring year that our country has no tradition which does it so much honour and which it should guard so jealously as that of its hospitality. It is a tradition that is unique as far as my experience goes (and I have visited not a few places abroad) among the modern nations.' This was Joyce's oblique way, in language that mocked his own, of beginning the task of making amends.

The selection of details for 'The Dead' shows Joyce making those choices which, while masterly, suggest the preoccupations that mastered him. Once he had determined to represent an Irish party, the choice of the Misses Morkans' as its location was easy enough. He had already reserved for *Stephen Hero* a Christmas party at his own house, a party which was also to be clouded by a discussion of a dead man. The other festive occasions of his childhood were associated with his hospitable great-aunts Mrs. Callanan and Mrs. Lyons, and Mrs. Callanan's daughter Mary Ellen, at their house at 15 Usher's Island, which

---

* The converse of this theme appears in *Ulysses* (113 [107]), when Bloom, walking in Glasnevin, thinks, "They are not going to get me this innings. Warm beds: warm fullblooded life.'
[5] Ibid. p. 48 (44).

was also known as the 'Misses Flynn school.'[6] There every year the Joyces who were old enough would go, and John Joyce carved the goose and made the speech. Stanislaus Joyce says that the speech of Gabriel Conroy in 'The Dead' is a good imitation of his father's oratorical style.*

In Joyce's story Mrs. Callanan and Mrs. Lyons, the Misses Flynn, become the spinster ladies, the Misses Morkan, and Mary Ellen Callanan becomes Mary Jane. Most of the other party guests were also reconstituted from Joyce's recollections. Mrs. Lyons had a son Freddy, who kept a Christmas card shop in Grafton Street.[7] Joyce introduces him as Freddy Malins, and situates his shop in the less fashionable Henry Street, perhaps to make him need that sovereign Gabriel lent him. Another relative of Joyce's mother, a first cousin, married a Protestant named Mervyn Archdale Browne, who combined the profession of music teacher with that of agent for a burglary insurance company. Joyce keeps him in 'The Dead' under his own name. Bartell d'Arcy, the hoarse singer in the story, was based upon Barton M'Guckin, the leading tenor in the Carl Rosa Opera Company. There were other tenors, such as John McCormack, whom Joyce might have used, but he needed one who was unsuccessful and uneasy about himself; and his father's often-told anecdote about M'Guckin's lack of confidence furnished him with just such a singer as he intended Bartell d'Arcy to be.

The making of his hero, Gabriel Conroy, was more complicated. The root situation, of jealousy for his wife's dead lover, was of course Joyce's. The man who is murdered, D. H. Lawrence has one of his characters say, desires to be murdered;[8] some temperaments demand the feeling that their friends and sweethearts will deceive them. Joyce's conversation often returned to the word 'betrayal,'[9] and the entangled innocents whom he uses for his heroes are all aspects of his conception of himself. Though Gabriel is less impressive than Joyce's other heroes, Stephen, Bloom, Richard Rowan, or Earwicker, he belongs to their distinguished, put-upon company.

There are several specific points at which Joyce attributes his own experiences to Gabriel. The letter which Gabriel remembers having written to Gretta Conroy early in their courtship is one of these; from it Gabriel quotes to himself the sentiment, 'Why is it that words like these seem to me so dull and cold? Is it because there is no word tender enough to be your name?' These sentences are taken almost directly from a letter Joyce wrote to Nora in 1904.[10] It was also Joyce, of course,

---

* He excepts the quotation from Browning, but even this was quite within the scope of the man who could quote Vergil when lending money to his son.
[6] Interview with Mrs. Joyce Monaghan, 1953.
[7] Idem.
[8] Birkin in *Women in Love*.
[9] Information from Professor Joseph Prescott.
[10] At Cornell.

who wrote book reviews, just as Gabriel Conroy does, for the *Daily Express.* Since the *Daily Express* was pro-English, he had probably been teased for writing for it during his frequent visits to the house of David Sheehy, M.P. One of the Sheehy daughters, Kathleen, may well have been the model for Miss Ivors, for she wore that austere bodice and sported the same patriotic pin.[12] In Gretta's old sweetheart, in Gabriel's letter, in the book reviews and the discussion of them, as well as in the physical image of Gabriel with hair parted in the middle and rimmed glasses, Joyce drew directly upon his own life.

His father was also deeply involved in the story. Stanislaus Joyce recalls that when the Joyce children were too young to bring along to the Misses Flynns' party, their father and mother sometimes left them with a governess and stayed at a Dublin hotel overnight instead of returning to their house in Bray.'[13] Gabriel and Gretta do this too. Gabriel's quarrels with his mother also suggest John Joyce's quarrels with his mother, who never accepted her son's marriage to a woman of lower station.[14] But John Joyce's personality was not like Gabriel's; he had no doubts of himself, in the midst of many failures he was full of self-esteem. He had the same unshakable confidence as his son James. For Gabriel's personality there is among Joyce's friends another model.[15] This was Constantine Curran, sometimes nicknamed 'Cautious Con.' He is a more distinguished man than Joyce allows, but Joyce was building upon, and no doubt distorting, his memories of Curran as a very young man. That he has Curran partly in mind is suggested by the fact that he calls Gabriel's brother by Curran's first name Constantine, and makes Gabriel's brother, like Curran's, a priest.[16] Curran has the same high color and nervous, disquieted manner as Gabriel, and like Gabriel he has traveled to the continent and has cultivated cosmopolitan interests. Curran, like Conroy, married a woman who was not a Dubliner, though she came from only as far west as Limerick. In other respects he is quite different. Gabriel was made mostly out of Curran, Joyce's father, and Joyce himself. Probably Joyce knew there was a publican on Howth named Gabriel Conroy; or, as Gerhard Friedrich has proposed,[17] he may have borrowed the name from the title of a Bret Harte novel. But the character, if not the name, was of his own compounding. (The name of Conroy's wife Gretta was borrowed from another friend, Gretta (actually Margaret) Cousins, the wife of James H. Cousins. Since Joyce mentioned in a letter at the same time that he

[12] Interview with Mrs. Mary Sheehy Kettle, 1953.
[13] *My Brother's Keeper,* p. 38 (58).
[14] See p. 17.
[15] Interview with S. Joyce, 1953.
[16] Suggested to me by Professor Vivian Mercier.
[17] Gerhard Friedrich, 'Bret Harte as a Source for James Joyce's "The Dead," ' *Philological Quarterly,* XXXIII (Oct. 1954), pp. 442–4.

was meditating 'The Dead,' the danger of becoming 'a patient Cousins,' this family was evidently on his mind.)[18]

Joyce now had his people, his party, and something of its development. In the festive setting, upon which the snow keeps offering a different perspective until, as W. Y. Tindall suggests,[19] the snow itself changes, he develops Gabriel's private tremors, his sense of inadequacy, his uncomfortable insistence on his small pretensions. From the beginning he is vulnerable; his well-meant and even generous overtures are regularly checked. The servant girl punctures his blithe assumption that everyone is happily in love and on the way to the altar. He is not sure enough of himself to put out of his head the slurs he has received long ago; so in spite of his uxorious attitude towards Gretta he is a little ashamed of her having come from the west of Ireland. He cannot bear to think of his dead mother's remark that Gretta was 'country cute,' and when Miss Ivors says of Gretta, 'She's from Connacht, isn't she?' Gabriel answers shortly, 'Her people are.' He has rescued her from that bog. Miss Ivors's suggestion, a true Gaelic Leaguer's, that he spend his holiday in the Irish-speaking Aran Islands (in the west) upsets him; it is the element in his wife's past that he wishes to forget. During most of the story, the west of Ireland is connected in Gabriel's mind with a dark and rather painful primitivism, an aspect of his country which he has steadily abjured by going off to the continent. The west is savagery; to the east and south lie people who drink wine and wear galoshes.

Gabriel has been made uneasy about this attitude, but he clings to it defiantly until the ending. Unknown to him, it is being challenged by the song, 'The Lass of Aughrim.' Aughrim is a little village in the west not far from Galway. The song has a special relevance; in it a woman who has been seduced and abandoned by Lord Gregory comes with her baby in the rain to beg for admission to his house. It brings together the peasant mother and the civilized seducer, but Gabriel does not listen to the words; he only watches his wife listening. Joyce had heard this ballad from Nora; perhaps he considered also using Tom Moore's 'O, Ye Dead' in the story, but if so he must have seen that 'The Lass of Aughrim' would connect more subtly with the west and with Michael Furey's visit in the rain to Gretta. But the notion of using a song at all may well have come to him as the result of the excitement generated in him by Moore's song.

And now Gabriel and Gretta go to the Hotel Gresham, Gabriel fired by his living wife and Gretta drained by the memory of her dead lover. He learns for the first time of the young man in Galway, whose name Joyce has deftly altered from Sonny or Michael Bodkin to Michael

[18] Letter to S. Joyce, Feb. 1907.
[19] W. Y. Tindall, The Literary Symbol (New York, 1955), p. 227.

Furey. The new name suggests, like the contrast of the militant Michael and the amiable Gabriel, that violent passion is in her Galway past, not in her Dublin present. Gabriel tries to cut Michael Furey down. 'What was he?' he asks, confident that his own profession of language teacher (which of course he shared with Joyce) is superior; but she replies, 'He was in the gasworks,' as if this profession was as good as any other. Then Gabriel tries again, 'And what did he die of so young, Gretta? Consumption, was it?' He hopes to register the usual expressions of pity, but Gretta silences and terrifies him by her answer, 'I think he died for me.'* Since Joyce has already made clear that Michael Furey was tubercular, this answer of Gretta has a fine ambiguity. It asserts the egoism of passion, and unconsciously defies Gabriel's reasonable question.

Now Gabriel begins to succumb to his wife's dead lover, and becomes a pilgrim to emotional intensities outside of his own experience. From a biographical point of view, these final pages compose one of Joyce's several tributes to his wife's artless integrity. Nora Barnacle, in spite of her defects of education, was independent, unself-conscious, instinctively right. Gabriel acknowledges the same coherence in his own wife, and he recognizes in the west of Ireland, in Michael Furey, a passion he has himself always lacked. 'Better pass boldly into that other world, in the full glory of some passion, than fade and wither dismally with age,' Joyce makes Gabriel think. Then comes that strange sentence in the final paragraph: 'The time had come for him to set out on his journey westward.' The cliché runs that journeys westward are towards death, but the west has taken on a special meaning in the story. Gretta Conroy's west is the place where life had been lived simply and passionately. The context and phrasing of the sentence suggest that Gabriel is on the edge of sleep, and half-consciously accepts what he has hitherto scorned, the possibility of an actual trip to Connaught. What the sentence affirms, at last, on the level of feeling, is the west, the primitive, untutored, impulsive country from which Gabriel had felt himself alienated before; in the story, the west is paradoxically linked also with the past and the dead. It is like Aunt Julia Morkan who, though ignorant, old, grey-skinned, and stupefied, seizes in her song at the party 'the excitement of swift and secure flight.'

The tone of the sentence, 'The time had come for him to set out on his journey westward,' is somewhat resigned. It suggests a concession, a relinquishment, and Gabriel is conceding and relinquishing a good

* Adaline Glasheen has discovered here an echo of Yeats's nationalistic play, *Cathleen ni Houlihan* (1902), where the old woman who symbolizes Ireland sings a song of 'yellow-haired Donough that was hanged in Galway.' When she is asked, 'What was it brought him to his death?' she replies, 'He died for love of me; many a man has died for love of me.' [20]

[20] I am indebted to Mrs. Glasheen for pointing this out to me.

deal—his sense of the importance of civilized thinking, of continental tastes, of all those tepid but nice distinctions on which he has prided himself. The bubble of his self-possession is pricked; he no longer possesses himself, and not to possess oneself is in a way a kind of death. It is a self-abandonment not unlike Furey's, and through Gabriel's mind runs the imagery of Calvary. He imagines the snow on the cemetery at Oughterard, lying 'thickly drifted on the crooked crosses and head-stones, on the spears of the little gate, on the barren thorns.' He thinks of Michael Furey who, Gretta has said, died for her, and envies him his sacrifice for another kind of love than Christ's. To some extent Gabriel too is dying for her, in giving up what he has most valued in himself, all that holds him apart from the simpler people at the party. He feels close to Gretta through sympathy if not through love; now they are both past youth, beauty, and passion; he feels close also to her dead lover, another lamb burnt on her altar, though she too is burnt now; he feels no resentment, only pity. In his own sacrifice of himself he is conscious of a melancholy unity between the living and the dead.

Gabriel, who has been sick of his own country, finds himself drawn inevitably into a silent tribute to it of much more consequence than his spoken tribute to the party. He has had illusions of the rightness of a way of life that should be outside of Ireland; but through this experi-ence with his wife he grants a kind of bondage, of acceptance, even of admiration to a part of the country and a way of life that are most Irish. Ireland is shown to be stronger, more intense than he. At the end of A Portrait of the Artist, too, Stephen Dedalus, who has been so reso-lutely opposed to nationalism, makes a similar concession when he interprets his departure from Ireland as an attempt to forge a conscience for his race.

Joyce did not invent the incidents that conclude his story, the sec-ond honeymoon of Gabriel and Gretta which ends so badly. His method of composition was very like T. S. Eliot's, the imaginative absorption of stray material. The method did not please Joyce very much because he considered it not imaginative enough, but it was the only way he could work. He borrowed the ending for 'The Dead' from another book. In that book a bridal couple receive, on their wedding night, a message that a young woman whom the husband jilted has just committed suicide. The news holds them apart, she asks him not to kiss her, and both are tormented by remorse. The wife, her marriage unconsum-mated, falls off at last to sleep, and her husband goes to the window and looks out at 'the melancholy greyness of the dawn.' For the first time he recognizes, with the force of a revelation, that his life is a failure, and that his wife lacks the passion of the girl who has killed herself. He resolves that, since he is not worthy of any more momentous career, he will try at least to make her happy. Here surely is the situa-tion that Joyce so adroitly recomposed. The dead lover who comes between the lovers, the sense of the husband's failure, the acceptance of mediocrity, the resolve to be at all events sympathetic, all come from the other book. But Joyce transforms them. For example, he allows Gretta to kiss her husband, but without desire, and rarefies the situation by having it arise not from a suicide but from a memory of young love. The book Joyce was borrowing from was one that nobody reads any more, George Moore's *Vain Fortune*; but Joyce read it,* and in his youthful essay, 'The Day of the Rabblement,' overpraised it as 'fine, original work.' [21]

Moore said nothing about snow, however. No one can know how Joyce conceived the joining of Gabriel's final experience with the snow. But his fondness for a background of this kind is also illustrated by his use of the fireplace in 'Ivy Day,' of the streetlamps in 'Two Gallants,' and of the river in *Finnegans Wake*. It does not seem that the snow can be death, as so many have said, for it falls on living and dead alike, and for death to fall on the dead is a simple redundancy of which Joyce would not have been guilty. For snow to be 'general all over Ireland' is of course unusual in that country. The fine description: 'It was falling on every part of the dark central plain, on the treeless hills, falling softly upon the Bog of Allen and, farther westward, softly falling into the dark mutinous Shannon waves,' is probably borrowed by Joyce from a famous simile in the twelfth book of the Iliad, which Thoreau translates: [22] 'The snowflakes fall thick and fast on a winter's day. The winds are lulled, and the snow falls incessant, covering the tops of the mountains, and the hills, and the plains where the lotus-tree grows, and the cultivated fields, and they are falling by the inlets and shores of the foaming sea, but are silently dissolved by the waves.' But Homer was simply describing the thickness of the arrows in the battle of the Greeks and Trojans; and while Joyce seems to copy his topographical details, he uses the image here chiefly for a similar sense of crowding and quiet pressure. Where Homer speaks of the waves silently dissolving the snow, Joyce adds the final detail of 'the mutinous Shannon waves' which suggests the 'Furey' quality of the west. The snow that falls upon Gabriel, Gretta, and Michael Furey, upon the Misses Morkan, upon the dead singers and the living, is mutuality, a sense of their connection with each other, a sense that none has his being alone. The partygoers prefer dead singers to living ones, the wife prefers a dead lover to a live lover.

---

* He evidently refreshed his memory of it when writing 'The Dead,' for his copy of *Vain Fortune*, now at Yale, bears the date 'March 1907.'

[21] *The Critical Writings of James Joyce*, eds. Ellsworth Mason and Richard Ellman (N. Y., 1959), p. 71.

[22] Professor Walter B. Rideout kindly called my attention to the similarity of these passages.

The snow does not stand alone in the story. It is part of the complex imagery that includes heat and cold air, fire, and rain, as well as snow. The relations of these are not simple. During the party the living people, their festivities, and all human society seem contrasted with the cold outside, as in the warmth of Gabriel's hand on the cold pane. But this warmth is felt by Gabriel as stuffy and confining, and the cold outside is repeatedly connected with what is fragrant and fresh. The cold, in this sense of piercing intensity culminates in the picture of Michael Furey in the rain and darkness of the Galway night.

Another warmth is involved in 'The Dead.' In Gabriel's memory of his own love for Gretta, he recalls incidents in his love's history as stars, burning with pure and distant intensity, and recalls moments of his passion for her as having the fire of stars. The irony of this image is that the sharp and beautiful experience was, though he has not known it until this night, incomplete. There is a telling metaphor: he remembers a moment of happiness, standing with Gretta in the cold, looking in through a window at a man making bottles in a roaring furnace, and suddenly calling out to the man, 'Is the fire hot?' The question sums up his naive deprivation; if the man at the furnace had heard the question, his answer, thinks Gabriel, might have been rude; so the revelation on this night is rude to Gabriel's whole being. On this night he acknowledges that love must be a feeling which he has never fully had.

Gabriel is not utterly deprived. Throughout the story there is affection for this man who, without the sharpest, most passionate perceptions, is yet generous and considerate. The intense and the moderate can meet; intensity bursts out and declines, and the moderated can admire and pity it, and share the fate that moves both types of mankind towards age and death. The furthest point of love of which Gabriel is capable is past. Furey's passion is past because of his sudden death. Gretta is perhaps the most pitiful, in that knowing Furey's passion, and being of his kind, she does not die but lives to wane in Gabriel's way; on this night she too is fatigued, not beautiful, her clothes lie crumpled beside her. The snow seems to share in this decline; viewed from inside at the party, it is desirable, unattainable, just as at his first knowledge of Michael Furey, Gabriel envies him. At the end as the partygoers walk to the cab the snow is slushy and in patches, and then, seen from the window of the hotel room, it belongs to all men, it is general, mutual. Under its canopy, all human beings, whatever their degrees of intensity, fall into union. The mutuality is that all men feel and lose feeling, all interact, all warrant the sympathy that Gabriel now extends to Furey, to Gretta, to himself, even to old Aunt Julia.

In its lyrical, melancholy acceptance of all that life and death offer, 'The Dead' is a linchpin in Joyce's work. There is that basic situation of cuckoldry, real or putative, which is to be found throughout. There is the special Joycean collation of specific detail raised to rhythmical intensity. The final purport of the story, the mutual dependency of living and dead, is something that he meditated a good deal from his early youth. He had expressed it first in his essay on Mangan in 1902, when he spoke already of the union in the great memory of death along with life;[23] even then he had begun to learn like Gabriel that we are all Romes, our new edifices reared beside, and even joined with, ancient monuments. In *Dubliners* he developed this idea. The interrelationship of dead and living is the theme of the first story in *Dubliners* as well as of the last; it is also the theme of 'A Painful Case,' but an even closer parallel to 'The Dead' is the story, 'Ivy Day in the Committee Room.' This was in one sense an answer to his university friends who mocked his remark that death is the most beautiful form of life by saying that absence is the highest form of presence. Joyce did not think either idea absurd. What binds 'Ivy Day' to 'The Dead' is that in both stories the central agitation derives from a character who never appears, who is dead, absent. Joyce wrote Stanislaus that Anatole France had given him the idea for both stories.[24] There may be other sources in France's works, but a possible one is 'The Procurator of Judaea.' In it Pontius Pilate reminisces with a friend about the days when he was procurator in Judaea, and describes the events of his time with Roman reason, calm, and elegance. Never once does he, or his friend, mention the person we expect him to discuss, the founder of Christianity, until at the end the friend asks if Pontius Pilate happens to remember someone of the name of Jesus, from Nazareth, and the veteran administrator replies, 'Jesus? Jesus of Nazareth? I cannot call him to mind.' The story is overshadowed by the person whom Pilate does not recall; without him the story would not exist. Joyce uses a similar method in 'Ivy Day' with Parnell and in 'The Dead' with Michael Furey.

In *Ulysses* the climactic episode, *Circe*, whirls to a sepulchral close in the same juxtaposition of living and dead, the ghost of his mother confronting Stephen, and the ghost of his son confronting Bloom. But Joyce's greatest triumph in asserting the intimacy of living and dead was to be the close of *Finnegans Wake*. Here Anna Livia Plurabelle, the river of life, flows toward the sea, which is death; the fresh water passes into the salt, a bitter ending. Yet it is also a return to her father, the sea, that produces the cloud which makes the river, and her father is also her husband, to whom she gives herself as a bride to her groom. Anna Livia is going back to her father, as Gabriel journeys westward in feeling to the roots of his fatherland; like him, she is sad and weary. To him the Shannon waves are dark and mutinous, and to her the sea is cold and mad. In *Finnegans Wake* Anna Livia's union is not only with love but with death; like Gabriel she seems to swoon away.

---

[23] *Critical Writings*, p. 83.
[24] Letter to S. Joyce, Feb. 11, 1907.

That Joyce at the age of twenty-five and -six should have written this story ought not to seem odd. Young writers reach their greatest eloquence in dwelling upon the horrors of middle age and what follows it. But beyond this proclivity which he shared with others, Joyce had a special reason for writing the story of 'The Dead' in 1906 and 1907. In his own mind he had thoroughly justified his flight from Ireland, but he had not decided the question of where he would fly to. In Trieste and Rome he had learned what he had unlearned in Dublin, to be a Dubliner. As he had written his brother from Rome with some astonishment, he felt humiliated when anyone attacked his 'impoverished country.'[25] 'The Dead' is his first song of exile.

[25] Letter to S. Joyce, Sept. 25, 1906.

QUESTIONS FOR DISCUSSION AND WRITING

1. The main import of Ellman's account of the backgrounds of *The Dead* is that Joyce's life helps to explain the story. What are some of the limitations in a biographical approach to *The Dead*? What are some of the advantages of knowing about such things as Sonny Bodkin and the annual Christmas dinner?

2. Retrace Ellmann's method of blending biographical information and critical analysis. What functions do the first six paragraphs serve? What specific details of character, symbol, and theme do successive paragraphs treat?

3. Cite some of the important parallels between Joyce and Gabriel. How do you think these parallels should effect our estimate of Gabriel's character?

4. Ellmann contends that Gabriel, though "less impressive," is nevertheless, one of Joyce's fictional "heroes." Presuming the validity of this view, what would you deduce as some of the characteristics of a Joycean "hero"?

5. How does Ellmann explain the meaning of the story's title—both in terms of its sources and in terms of its thematic significance?

6. Ellmann says, "The cliché runs that journeys westward are towards death." To what "cliché" is he referring? Can you cite any examples of the use of the west in literature as a symbol of a journey toward death? Any instances of the west having a different symbolic value? What does Ellmann feel the west symbolizes in this story?

RECOLLECTIONS OF JAMES JOYCE*

Stanislaus Joyce

Joyce refused the position of assistant professor at the University, but he accepted a very low-paid position in a little private school near Dublin. In addition, he wrote book reviews for a Dublin newspaper. . . .

At Russell's request, he began to send to the *Irish Homestead* the first of those stories which were later included in *Dubliners*. This agricultural magazine, which had a circulation in the country, wanted to publish a short-story every week, and Russell suggested something humorous, sentimental, or romantic. Before leaving Dublin, Joyce wrote three stories, but the editor-in-chief of this little magazine for country folk was not satisfied with them. He said that he acknowledged the author's brilliant style, but he did not see much originality in the stories.

The influence of Maupassant on Joyce's short-stories is often pointed out. Joyce admired the works of Maupassant, but he objected that the French writer is at times too concise because of his insistent wish to define things in a phrase and that he was frequently brutal in judging the characters of his stories. His stories always tell some anecdote which is amusing, indecent, pathetic, or brutal, and in the course of which the life of the characters seems to rise to a momentary interest only to fall back again into banality, where the author follows it no longer. In Joyce's stories, on the other hand, the everyday life of the characters interests him, and the incident, in itself so slight that it hardly warrants being called an incident, serves only to illuminate a certain moment of the everyday life. Judgment is always suspended. The author's one duty is to narrate; assumptions and inquiries he keeps to himself, or, if they do peep forth on rare occasions, they are unexpected and profound.

In Joyce, a literary conscience had been substituted for a religious conscience. He turned from the word of God to the spoken word with undiminished intransigence and meticulousness. He insisted on the necessity of simple hard work in writing; and up to the very end, in spite of his half-blindness, he continued to write, with the aid of a

* Reprinted from *Recollections of James Joyce* by Stanislaus Joyce, by permission of The James Joyce Society.

magnifying glass. During his first eye ailment in Trieste, he dictated to me the ending of his story The Dead. During the evening, when I had time at my disposal, he would dictate what he had composed in his mind during the day, but in general he did not like to dictate lest he should become facile. The final drafts of his manuscripts contained no corrections. He was not an inspirational writer who had to wait for the impulse of the moment; he knew the "fine frenzy" of the poet, but he dominated it and made it serve his purpose. He often quoted lines from a poem of Ibsen which says, more or less, "to write poetry means to hold Judgment Day over ourselves." Joyce worked with tireless patience; above all, with patience. Sometimes when speaking to me he would burst out against someone, and I would say to him, "Now where is this patience that you boast about?" He would reply, "But I didn't write it," and then, speaking of himself in the third person, he would add ironically, "when the bard begins to write, he intellectualizes himself."

The story The Dead is also, in its way, a story of ghosts, of the dead who return in envy of the living. In this story, which is the finest of the group, the dead man is only a memory, but a memory so alive and dominant that it spoils the festivities of the living. In describing a dance and the supper which follows it, Joyce works page after page in minute detail to create the atmosphere of little bourgeois beings who are noisy, vulgar, and harmless. As the festivities are drawing to a close and the laughter is at its height, the voice of someone singing an old Irish air, barely audible in the distance, recalls vividly to a woman's memory a true romantic passion which had been extinguished in death; and the remembrance of it annihilates at a stroke her own happiness and that of the principal character of the story. Then gradually the noise of the festivities, and the passions, and the living memory of the dead, are allayed in sleep.

QUESTIONS FOR DISCUSSION AND WRITING

1. Stanislaus Joyce says his brother was asked to provide "humorous, sentimental, or romantic" short stories. What might be some examples of these qualities? How close does The Dead come to providing any of these qualities?

2. Stanislaus emphasizes the neutrality of his brother, condemning Maupassant for "judging the characters of his stories." Stanislaus further claims, "Judgment is always suspended" in his brother's fiction. How is this true? Are there any "judgments" made in The Dead? How do his remarks about judgment fit in with his comment about the characters of The Dead being "noisy, vulgar and harmless"?

3. Stanislaus says his brother substituted "a literary conscience" for "a religious conscience." How does he describe a "literary conscience"?

4. What are some of the ramifications of Stanislaus's comment that The Dead is "a story of ghosts"?

SHE WEEPS OVER RAHOON*

James Joyce

EDITOR'S NOTE

Interesting references to *The Dead* show up in several letters Joyce wrote after having completed the story. The first reference comes in 1909 when, as Ellmann says, "Joyce, like Gabriel Conroy, was now making the journey westward and thereby tacitly granting the hold over him of the past." While in Ireland in 1909, Joyce visited Galway, the home of his wife, Nora. During the visit with his wife's family, Joyce prevailed upon Mrs. Barnacle, Nora's mother, to sing the whole of "The Lass of Aughrim."

In letters to his wife during this period there are two references of interest to readers of *The Dead*. On the 22nd of August Joyce wrote:

> Do you remember the three adjectives I have used in 'The Dead' in speaking of your body. They are these: 'musical and strange and perfumed.'

On the 31st of August he wrote:

> I was singing an hour ago your song, The Lass of Aughrim. The tears come into my eays and my voice trembles with emotion when I sing that lovely air.[1]

In 1912 Joyce visited Ireland for the last time and, once again, themes and references to *The Dead* are prominent. During this visit Joyce journeyed to the western-most part of Ireland—the Aran Islands, the islands that Miss Ivors urged Gabriel to visit in *The Dead*. Joyce

---

* From *Pomes Penyeach* by James Joyce. Copyright 1927 by James Joyce. Reprinted by permission of the Viking Press, Inc.

[1] These two quotations are from The Joyce Collection, Cornell University Library, and are used with permission of the Library and the Society of Authors. A perceptive discussion of Joyce's relationship to Nora as revealed in the whole collection of letters he wrote to her during this period appears in "Joyce and Nora: The Indispensable Countersign," by Mary T. Reynolds, *Sewanee Review* (Winter, 1964), pp. 29–64. The student might find Mrs. Reynolds' discussion useful for comparison with the Gabriel-Gretta relationship.

wrote accounts of his visit for an Italian newspaper. These accounts reveal Joyce as an observant and sympathetic traveler.[2]

Also during this visit, on which Nora accompanied Joyce, they visited the grave of Michael Bodkin—Nora's childhood sweetheart. Closely associated with this visit is Joyce's poem, "She Weeps Over Rahoon." Ellmann comments on Joyce's visit to the cemetery at Rahoon in Galway: "With a sense of sacred coincidence Joyce found a headstone at Rahoon with the name of J. Joyce upon it, an occult verification of the journey westward of Gabriel in 'The Dead'."

SHE WEEPS OVER RAHOON

Rain on Rahoon falls softly, softly falling,
Where my dark lover lies.
Sad is his voice that calls me, sadly calling,
At grey moonrise.

Love, hear thou
How soft, how sad his voice is ever calling,
Ever unanswered and the dark rain falling,
Then as now.

Dark too our hearts, O love, shall lie and cold
As his sad heart has lain
Under the moongrey nettles, the black mould
And muttering rain.

QUESTIONS FOR DISCUSSION AND WRITING

1. Clarify as precisely as possible the identity of the speaker in this poem. What essentially does she say? What are the circumstances of her utterance? Are her "statements" addressed to another, or are her "statements" simply overheard thoughts?

2. Is there any development or progression in the thought of the poem? How are the ideas and circumstances of this poem related to The Dead?

3. What is the symbolic value of the rain in this poem? Is there any symbolic relationship to The Dead? Are there any techniques of language evident here which recall techniques of The Dead?

4. From your brief comparison of this poem with the short story, make some observations about how poetry and prose deal with similar emotional experiences.

[2] Two accounts of Joyce's trip to the west of Ireland, translated from the Italian, appear in The Critical Writing of James Joyce, ed. Ellsworth Mason and Richard Ellmann (N.Y., 1959), pp. 229–233, 234–237.

JOYCE'S LETTER TO HENRIK IBSEN*

March 1901   8 *Royal Terrace, Fairfield, Dublin*

Honoured Sir: I write to you to give you greeting on your seventy-third birthday and to join my voice to those of your well-wishers in all lands. You may remember that shortly after the publication of your latest play, *When We Dead Awaken,* an appreciation of it appeared in one of the English reviews—*The Fortnightly Review*—over my name. I know that you have seen it because some short time afterwards Mr William Archer wrote to me and told me that in a letter he had had from you some days before, you had written, 'I have read or rather spelled out a review in *The Fortnightly Review* by Mr James Joyce which is very benevolent and for which I should greatly like to thank the author if only I had sufficient knowledge of the language.' (My own knowledge of your language is not, as you see, great but I trust you will be able to decipher my meaning.') I can hardly tell you how moved I was by your message. I am a young, a very young man, and perhaps the telling of such tricks of the nerves will make you smile. But I am sure if you go back along your own life to the time when you were an undergraduate at the University as I am, and if you think what it would have meant to you to have earned a word from one who held as high a place in your esteem as you hold in mine, you will understand my feeling. One thing only I regret, namely, that an immature and hasty article should have met your eye rather than something better and worthier of your praise. There may not have been any wilful stupidity in it, but truly I can say no more. It may annoy you to have your works at the mercy of striplings but I am sure you would prefer hotheadedness to nerveless and 'cultured' paradoxes.

What shall I say more? I have sounded your name defiantly through the college where it was either unknown or known faintly and darkly. I have claimed for you your rightful place in the history of the drama.

---

[1] Gorman in his biography states that Joyce wrote the letter first in English and then turned it into Norwegian.

* From *Letters of James Joyce* edited by Stuart Gilbert. Copyright © 1957 by The Viking Press, Inc. Reprinted by permission of The Viking Press, Inc. and The Society of Authors.

I have shown what, as it seemed to me, was your highest excellence—your lofty impersonal power. Your minor claims—your satire, your technique and orchestral harmony—these, too, I advanced. Do not think me a hero-worshipper—I am not so. And when I spoke of you in debating societies and so forth, I enforced attention by no futile ranting.

But we always keep the dearest things to ourselves. I did not tell them what bound me closest to you. I did not say how what I could discern dimly of your life was my pride to see, how your battles inspired me—not the obvious material battles but those that were fought and won behind your forehead, how your wilful resolution to wrest the secret from life gave me heart and how in your absolute indifference to public canons of art, friends and shibboleths you walked in the light of your inward heroism. And this is what I write to you of now. Your work on earth draws to a close and you are near the silence. It is growing dark for you. Many write of such things, but they do not know. You have only opened the way—though you have gone as far as you could upon it—to the end of 'John Gabriel Borkman' and its spiritual truth—but your last play stands, I take it, apart. But I am sure that higher and holier enlightenment lies—onward.

As one of the young generation for whom you have spoken I give you greeting—not humbly, because I am obscure and you in the glare, not sadly, because you are an old man and I am a young man, not presumptuously nor sentimentally—but joyfully, with hope and with love, I give you greeting.

QUESTIONS FOR DISCUSSION AND WRITING

1. What sense of Joyce's young personality (he had just turned nineteen) does this letter convey?

2. Joyce writes: "Do not think me a hero-worshipper—I am not so." Why does he try to protect himself against such a charge? Does he appear to be "hero-worshipping"?

3. What essential spirit in Ibsen did Joyce find most congenial?

IBSEN, JOYCE, AND THE LIVING-DEAD*

James R. Baker

In 1900 Joyce wrote two essays in which he announced an unqualified admiration for Ibsen's later plays. The first, "Drama and Life," dismisses the Greek and Elizabethan traditions as outmoded and praises Ibsen for finding "the deathless passions" amid the commonplaces of modern bourgeois existence. "Ibsen's New Drama," the second, is an eulogistic review of *When We Dead Awaken*, which concludes that appreciation is the only fitting response to the "perfect" dramatist and "one of the world's great men." "The Day of the Rabblement" and the famous letter to Ibsen, both written the following year, continue with unchecked enthusiasm. According to Richard Ellmann's biography, Joyce carried his crusade to the Continent where he frequently defended Ibsen or sought to win new admirers. As late as 1936 (during the last stages of work on *Finnegans Wake*) we find him accepting with delight a comparison between Ibsen and himself, on another occasion insisting that Ibsen is "head and shoulders" above Shakespeare, and on still another arguing with James Stephens over the merits of *Little Eyolf*.[1]

The influence of Ibsen on the theme and structure of *Exiles* is a long-established recognition in Joycean criticism.[2] In his chapter on "The Backgrounds of 'The Dead' " Ellmann extends the range of influence by sketching the presence of Ibsen's resurrection motif in a few of the stories of *Dubliners* and in all subsequent work, but the natural association of drama with drama continues to support the notion that the play is the only really blatant example of Joyce's debt.

By the end of 1914 Joyce had published *Chamber Music*, finished *Dubliners, Portrait of the Artist*, and *Exiles*, as well as the early plans for *Ulysses*. In a period of fourteen years, then, he conceived his basic subjects and techniques. It would be surprising to find that his regard for Ibsen had a significant function only in the case of the play. I wish to argue here that *Dubliners* affords not only an earlier but an even more

---

* From *A James Joyce Miscellany: Third Series* edited by Marvin Magalaner. Copyright © 1962 by Southern Illinois University Press. Reprinted by permission of the Southern Illinois University Press.

[1] Richard Ellmann, *James Joyce* (New York, 1959), pp. 701, 707, 709–10.

[2] James T. Farrell, "*Exiles* and Ibsen," in *James Joyce: Two Decades of Criticism*, ed. Seon Givens (New York, 1948), pp. 95–131; Francis Fergusson, "A Reading of *Exiles*" (Preface), *Exiles* (Norfolk, Connecticut, 1945), pp. v-xviii.

radical example than *Exiles.* Like Ibsen's "social" dramas, *Dubliners* is an exposé of the paralysis of spirit which binds the urban bourgeois. Less obvious, the basic themes, the structural design, and symbolism of the stories parallel Ibsen's work in the group of plays beginning with *A Doll's House* and ending with *When We Dead Awaken.* The last play is most crucial because it provided for Joyce a neatly condensed version of the symbolic parable he was to repeat all his life, from *Chamber Music* through *Finnegans Wake.*

In his review of *When We Dead Awaken* Joyce notes that this play is the final member in a succession of eleven works dealing with "modern life," "a grand epilogue to its ten predecessors." For Ibsen it was the culmination of a theme which had occupied him at least twenty years—the vital ranges of experience beyond the lifeless region of the bourgeoisie and the problem for the artist of striking a balance between the dangers of rigid isolation and debilitating involvement. Joyce finds in it the embodiment of his own preoccupations: the problem of the artist's relationship to a spiritually mean society, the penalties of aloofness from the common stream of life, and, most pertinent for the stories shaping in his mind, a comprehensive dramatization of the pitiful failure of men to awaken from the somnolence which holds them among the living-dead.

Joyce begins his summary of the plot by pointing out that it is composed of a series of dialogues in which the major characters, the sculptor Rubeck and his former model, Irene, produce in each other the realization that they have "forfeited" their lives: Rubeck, for the sake of his art; Irene, because she has held herself aloof in an unrequited passion for Rubeck. The result is that both are essentially "dead." The same failure is immanent in the psychology of the minor figures, Maia, Rubeck's young and bored wife, and Ulfheim, the bitter recluse who has been rejected by his beloved. The two sets of characters form a counterpoint built upon the single theme of resurrection. Joyce demonstrates his complete understanding by selecting for quotation the lines which most clearly define the burden of a complex and (at least in the William Archer translation) heavily sentimental play:

> *Irene:* We see the irretrievable only when *(breaks short off).*
> *Rubeck: (looks inquiringly at her).* When?
> *Irene:* When we dead awaken.[3]

From the concluding scenes he adeptly chooses the following:

> *Irene:* The love that belongs to the life of earth—the beautiful, miraculous life of earth—the inscrutable life of earth—that is dead in both of us.
> *Rubeck: (throwing his arms violently about her).* Then let two of the dead—us two—for once live life to its uttermost, before we go down to our graves again.

[3] The passages from the play are cited by Joyce in "Ibsen's New Drama," *The Critical Writings*, eds. Ellsworth Mason and Richard Ellmann (New York, 1959), pp. 59, 61.

In his analysis of the characters the reviewer offers an interpretation of Rubeck which is something of a departure from Ibsen's obvious projection of himself—the aging artist who realizes too late the price of isolation and dedication to aesthetic motives. "Arnold Rubeck," comments Joyce, "is not intended to be a genius, as perhaps Eljert Lovbörg [in *Hedda Gabler*] is. Had he been a genius like Eljert he would have understood in a truer way the value of his life. But . . . the facts that he is devoted to his art and that he has attained to a degree of mastery in it—mastery of hand linked with limitation of thought—tells us that *there may be lying dormant in him a capacity for greater life, which may be exercised when he, a dead man, shall have risen from among the dead"* [4] (italics mine). Thus Rubeck's masterpiece, a statue called "The Ressurection," becomes the ironic symbol of the divorce between his art and his life. His personal resurrection comes too late, on the eve of his death. As he ascends the "Peak of Promise" with Irene, they are buried in the descending snow of an avalanche.

I have italicized the final portion of Joyce's comment on Rubeck because it defines with faultless precision the status of the characters in *Dubliners*. Most of them are summoned by these words: the boy of "The Sisters" and "Araby," Eveline, Little Chandler, Maria, Mr. Duffy, the wardmen of "Ivy Day in the Committee Room," and Gabriel Conroy. Each of these is "an outcast from life's feast," a member of the great host of the living-dead. For Joyce, as for Ibsen, "the timeless passions" are "lying dormant" in these drab lives. The Norwegian master offered eleven plays; Joyce offers fifteen miniature dramas on the same theme. Commenting on the relations between drama and modern life, the young essayist of 1900 formulates a statement of the aesthetic motives he was to pursue so consistently in *Dubliners*. "Still I think out of the dreary sameness of existence, a measure of dramatic life may be drawn. Even the most commonplace, the deadest among the living, may play a part in a great drama." [5] Thus the real unity of *Dubliners* derives from the condensed symbolism of Ibsen's last play. The technique of epiphany is only a means to an end, the pattern of eastward and westward movements[6] only an adjunct to the Ibsenesque juxtaposition of life and death, and the Homeric counterparts[7] (if they exist at all) are occasional analogies which function within the larger scheme provided by the dramatist's example.

When We Dead Awaken utilizes the same key metaphor which in one form or another appears in its predecessors—the comparison of the unawakened living with the dead. In *A Doll's House* Nora's existence is

[4] *Ibid.*, pp. 65–66.
[5] "Drama and Life," *The Critical Writings*, p. 45.
[6] Brewster Ghiselin, "The Unity of Joyce's *Dubliners*," *Accent*, XVI (Spring 1956), 75–88, and (Summer 1956), 196–213.
[7] Richard Levin and Charles Shattuck, "First Flight to Ithaca," in *James Joyce: Two Decades of Criticism*, pp. 47–94.

clearly a living death. Mrs. Alving of *Ghosts* adheres to a restrictive and Puritanical code of moral duties which prevents her from entering into a vital life. Paralyzed herself, she thus becomes responsible for the passionate indulgences of her husband and the consequent death of both husband and son. The dormant passions of Solness, the architect of *The Master Builder*, are awakened by the lively Hilda. In a strange final scene he escapes from the shroud which practical and moral demands have closed about him, and at the moment of his death rises to his former greatness.

It is obvious that Joyce adopted for *Dubliners* the basic metaphor which pervades this entire group of plays. But he also borrowed from them a device which is commonly traced to another source, his Catholic training. It was in Ibsen, however, that he found the basis for the technique of "epiphany." *When We Dead Awaken* is characteristic in its structure—a pattern in which the central character, through the stress of some unexpected crisis, is driven to an epiphanaic moment that reveals him as spiritually dead. The same structural design is typical of the stories in *Dubliners*. In "Araby" and "A Painful Case," for example, the initial vignette of paralysis is followed by an excruciating denouement in which reality rushes in upon the unprepared consciousness of the central character. Where the revelation is for the reader alone ("Two Gallants" or "Grace"), the persistent ironic metaphor emerges in a climactic scene. Conditioned by his Christian education, Joyce calls the instant of perception "epiphany," and so underscores the saving quality of a revelation containing the seeds not only of suffering but resurrection. While his term is clearly borrowed from the Christian context, the applied technique of epiphany is an adaptation of the structural principle common to Ibsen's dramas. It is worth noting that Joyce wrote most of the short sketches he called "Epiphanies" in a three year period beginning in 1900, at the very same time he was absorbing Ibsen's work. One of the "Epiphanies" is about Ibsen himself. And some of them image situations which foreshadow the stories in *Dubliners:* A "sudden spiritual manifestation" reveals the drabness or vulgarity of things, a latent passion for freedom, an abrupt awakening to life's possibilities.[8] Psychological suffering during the experience of epiphany and the promise of belated resurrection (so common in *Dubliners*) is stock Ibsen. One can imagine the delight with which Joyce discovered in the plays a convergence of the Christian, the secular, and the aesthetic.

He must have found equally appealing the rich irony which Ibsen develops again and again by allowing the voices of the dead to inform the living-dead. In *A Doll's House*, for example, the very presence of Dr.

---

[8] See *Epiphanies*, edited with an introduction and notes by O. A. Silverman (Buffalo, New York, 1956). [Some of these are given on pp. 83–85 of this casebook. Ed.]

Rank in the Helmer household stresses the urgency of Nora's awakening. Rank is fated to live with the knowledge that he must soon die. Afflicted with a steadily advancing paralysis, a heritage from his father's indulgences, he adores beauty and vitality. On the eve of his death, he tells Nora of his love for her. Thus do the lost and ghostly passions of the dead become the agents of resurrection. Hedda Gabler's suicide follows quickly upon her recognition that the dead Lövborg embodies the passionate creativity which is foreign to the listless bourgeoisdom she inhabits. The device is characteristic, and examples can be multiplied.

With ingenious variation Joyce employs in *Dubliners* the same means of achieving irony and pathos. And just as in Ibsen the effect is to reinforce, either for the reader or a character suffering epiphany, the comparison of living and dead. In both "The Sisters" and "Araby" the frightening portent of paralysis and death is represented in the figure of a dead priest, and in each case it provokes in the child a bid for escape. Eveline, appalled by the fate of her dead mother, attempts to break out but fails. In "A Painful Case" the ghost of Emily Sinico illuminates for Duffy his outcast state and his status as one of the living-dead. A similar humiliation comes to Gabriel Conroy as his aerial and frigid soul is chastened by the visit of Michael Furey.

If we consider the problem which occupied Joyce's youth—his passionate quest for freedom from home, fatherland, and church—the appeal of Ibsen seems inevitable. In the invidious metaphor which dominates the later plays, and in the dramatic evolution designed to torture and expose bourgeois lassitude, Joyce found confirmation of his personal and aesthetic motives. On the very eve of exile, as he prepared to encounter "the reality of experience" and resolved to forge "the uncreated conscience" of his race, he found in Ibsen the techniques that were to carry him to fulfillment. Within the Ibsen framework he saw the possibility of indulging all his predilections: his delight in ironic humor, his nearly obsessive awareness of the pathos of smothered potentials and dreams, his Jesuit penchant for moral analysis and categorizing, and, under the aegis of dramatic "objectivity," an opportunity for persecution of "the most belated race in Europe."

Interpretation of *Dubliners* in the light of the Ibsen parable often resolves points of disagreement among the commentators.[9] The early dismissal of the collection as an example of pure naturalism has given way (and properly so) to close analysis and the search for a pervading and unifying symbolism. The usual conclusion is that the symbology stems mainly if not exclusively from Joyce's Catholic background. Some of the interpretations offered on this basis are useful, but where Joyce utilizes the Christian paraphernalia it functions at a secondary level and

---

[9] A selected checklist of criticism of the individual stories, compiled by Maurice Beebe and Walton Litz, appears in *Modern Fiction Studies*, IV (Spring 1958), 83–85.

within the dominant Ibsen scheme. The two converge in *Dubliners*, and they meet again in all the subsequent works. Every story in *Dubliners* depends to one degree or another on the Ibsen formula, but the most subtle uses of his example appear in stories where there is little or no consciously articulated epiphany. . . .

"The Dead" was apparently written last, but it was certainly not "appended" to the volume merely for the purpose of toning down the biting judgments of the earlier pieces. Its great quality lies in the nearly perfect manipulation of the basic metaphor and technique which function throughout the volume. It is the culmination of a sustained and unified effort. With "The Dead" Joyce's skill comes to maturity, and we have a fully realized prose drama that equals or excels the art of his master. This is not to say that all of the other stories are inferior, but the characters who inhabit them constitute a limitation which inhibits the complete realization of possibilities latent in Joyce's subject. Since the characters do not achieve a significant degree of self-awareness, the epiphany cannot be fully articulated. And in keeping with the restraint of "dramatic" presentation, it must be rendered by the arrangement of ironies inherent in the various situations. These facts account for the obscurity and ambiguity in some of the stories. The effects are often over-subtle, the suggestions too frail to bear a maximum of implication. Thus most of the characters are pathetic but not tragic creatures. The young boy of the first three sketches merely intuits the nature of his environment; the adolescents of the next four either capitulate at the moment of crisis or remain unconscious of their peril; among the adults only Mr. Duffy and Gabriel Conroy drink a full measure of bitters; and all the participants in community affairs (from the priests and politicians down to the *artistes*) are hopelessly impervious.

"A Painful Case" and "The Dead" are notable exceptions because the two intelligences which dominate them make it possible for Joyce to arrive at a dignified and explicit articulation of the tragic dimension implicit in his design. For the same reason they contain the most obvious applications of the Ibsen theme and technique. "A Painful Case," however, is inferior to the final story. Though Mr. Duffy comes to realize his blindness and his guilt, his epiphany does not carry him beyond the borders of his own life; it leaves him an "outcast," living utterly alone, cut off even from the communion of suffering. The superior range and development of "The Dead" is possible because Gabriel Conroy has the intelligence and the imaginative vision to extend the implications of his own epiphany and so perceive the universal tragedy involving "all the living and the dead." His provincial ego dissolves, and in the twilight of that demise he sees that the indifferent snow descends over the entire cosmos of souls. In Gabriel's evolution one can measure the widening arc of Joyce's own perspective, the fruit of his studied apprenticeship to Ibsen.

QUESTIONS FOR DISCUSSION AND WRITING

1. Baker says that Joyce regarded " 'appreciation' as the only fitting response to the 'perfect' dramatist." Joyce had written: "Appreciation, hearkening is the only true criticism. . . . When the art of a dramatist is perfect the critic is superfluous." Discuss Joyce's critical criteria in general, and specifically in regard to The Dead.

2. What use does Baker make of Ellmann's comments on Ibsen? Do you find his acknowledgment of Ellmann's earlier work sufficient?

3. In Baker's plot summary of "When We Dead Awaken" what points strike you as most immediately relevant to Joyce's short story?

4. How does Baker interpret the symbolism of west in The Dead?

5. Baker refers to "the Ibsen framework," "Ibsen scheme," and "the Ibsen formula." How convincing is Baker's thesis that the Ibsen influence is the dominant influence on Joyce—particularly in The Dead.

6. Discuss Baker's idea that fictional characters may "constitute a limitation which inhibits the complete realization of possibilities latent" in a story.

7. Baker says: "Interpretation of Dubliners in light of . . . Ibsen . . . often resolves points of disagreement among the commentators." Analyze his remark and apply it to points of disagreement that you have already noticed.

A REVIEW OF *DUBLINERS* (1914)*

Gerald Gould

It is easy to say of Gorky that he is a man of genius. To say the same of Mr. James Joyce requires more courage, since his name is little known; but a man of genius is precisely what he is. He has an original outlook, a special method, a complete reliance on his own powers of delineation and presentment. Whether his powers will develop, his scope widen, his sympathies deepen, or not—whether, in short, his genius is a large one or only a little one, I cannot pretend to say. Maturity and self-confidence in a first book (and I believe that, in prose, this is Mr. Joyce's first book) contain a threat as well as a promise. They hint at a set mode of thought rather than a developing capacity. Certainly the maturity, the individual poise and force of these stories are astonishing. The only recent work with which they suggest comparison is *The House with the Green Shutters*, and even that was very different, for one heard in it the undertone of human compalint—its horrors were partly by way of expressing a personal unhappiness; while Mr. Joyce seems to regard this objective and dirty and crawling world with the cold detachment of an unamiable god.

He has plenty of humour, but it is always the humour of the fact, not of the comment. He dares to let people speak for themselves with the awkward meticulousness, the persistent incompetent repetition, of actual human intercourse. If you have never realised before how direly our daily conversation needs editing, you will realise it from Mr. Joyce's pages. One very powerful story, called *Grace,* consists chiefly of lengthy talk so banal, so true to life, that one can scarcely endure it—though one can still less leave off reading it. Here is one of the liveliest passages:

> "Pope Leo XIII.," said Mr. Cunningham, "was one of the lights of the age. His great idea, you know, was the union of the Latin and Greek churches. That was the aim of his life."
>
> "I often heard he was one of the most intellectual men in Europe," said Mr. Power. "I mean apart from his being Pope."
>
> "So he was," said Mr. Cunningham, "if not *the* most so. His motto, you know, as Pope was *Lux upon Lux—Light upon Light.*"
>
> "No, no," said Mr. Fogarty eagerly. "I think you're wrong there. It was *Lux in Tenebris,* I think—*Light in Darkness.*"
>
> "O yes," said Mr. M'Coy, "*Tenebrae.*"

* From *The New Statesman*, III (June 27, 1914), 374–375.

"Allow me," said Mr. Cunningham positively, "it was *Lux upon Lux*. And Pius IX. his predecessor's motto was *Crux upon Crux*—that is, *Cross upon Cross*—to show the difference between their two pontificates."

The inference was allowed. Mr. Cunningham continued.

"Pope Leo, you know, was a great scholar and a poet."

"He had a strong face," said Mr. Kernan.

"Yes," said Mr. Cunningham. "He wrote Latin poetry."

"Is that so?" said Mr. Fogarty.

You see the method? It is not employed only in conversation. The description of mood, of atmosphere, is just as detailed and just as relentless. Horrible sordid realities, of which you are not spared one single pang, close in upon you like the four walls of a torture-chamber. It is all done quite calmly, quite dispassionately, quite competently. It never bores. You sometimes rather wish it did, as a relief.

The best things in the book are *Araby*, a wonderful magical study of boyish affection and wounded pride, and *The Dead*, a long story (placed at the end) in which we begin with a queer old-fashioned dance, where the principal anxiety is whether a certain guest will arrive "screwed," and are led on through all the queer breathless banalities of supper and conversation and leave-taking till we find ourselves back with a husband and wife in their hotel bedroom, the husband's emotion stirred, the wife queerly remote and sad, remembering the boy, Michael Furey, whom she had loved and who had died because of her. To quote the end without the innumerable preparatory touches that prepare for it seems unfair; yet it must be quoted for its mere melancholy beauty:

A few light taps upon the pane made him turn to the window. It had begun to snow again. He watched sleepily the flakes, silver and dark, falling obliquely against the lamplight. The time had come for him to set out on his journey westward. Yes, the newspapers were right: snow was general all over Ireland. It was falling on every part of the dark central plain, on the treeless hills, falling softly upon the Bog of Allen and, farther westward, softly falling into the dark mutinous Shannon waves. It was falling, too, upon every part of the lonely churchyard on the hill where Michael Furey lay buried. It lay thickly drifted on the crooked crosses and headstones, on the spears of the little gate, on the barren thorns. His soul swooned slowly as he heard the snow falling faintly through the universe and faintly falling, like the descent of their last end, upon all the living and the dead.

Frankly, we think it a pity (perhaps we betray a narrow puritanism in so thinking) that a man who can write like this should insist as constantly as Mr. Joyce insists upon aspects of life which are ordinarily not mentioned. To do him justice, we do not think it is a pose with him: he simply includes the "unmentionable" in his persistent regard.

QUESTIONS FOR DISCUSSION AND WRITING

1. Why does Gould call the "little known" Joyce a man of genius? How does his opinion compare with more recent Joyce criticism? What effect does it have on a modern reader to see *Dubliners* compared with *The House with the Green Shutters*?

2. What does Gould mean by "the humour of the fact, not of the comment"? Why is the quoted dialogue both humorous and a good example of the banality of actual conversation? Can you recall a specific example of a conversation of this sort?

3. What does this reviewer have to say specifically about *The Dead*? How much evidence does he give to prove that the story is one of "the best things in the book"?

4. Despite the fact that Gould recognizes Joyce's genius, he nevertheless regrets some of the uses to which Joyce put his genius. What does he regret? How justified do you feel his regret is?

DUBLINERS*

William York Tindall

Dubliners consists of fifteen stories about Dubliners. Though each of these stories has a beginning, a middle, and an end, some seem lacking in conventional shape or import; yet, however unlike those in popular magazines, these stories are of a kind more or less familiar since the time of Chekhov. Lacking in obvious action maybe, the stories of Dubliners disclose human situations, moments of intensity. Each moves toward a moral, social, or spiritual revelation. To the simple reader, deceived by surfaces, Joyce's stories may seem simple, but they are not so simple as they seem. To the ingenious reader, these stories, though complicated enough, may seem more complicated than they are. Simplicity is the reader's Scylla and ingenuity his Charybdis. Our prudent course lying somewhere betwixt and between, we must try to see these fifteen things exactly as they are.

What holds them together and makes them a book—or one at least of the controlling priciples—is a theme or common idea. Hinted on the first page of Dubliners and displayed in the last story, this theme is "paralysis" or living death. That paralysis was meant to be the central word and a clue to meaning is confirmed by Joyce himself, who, in a letter of 1904, said he intended Dubliners "to betray the soul of that . . . paralysis which many consider a city." His stories, faithful to his intention, betray impotence, frustration, and death. His city is the heart of paralysis and all the citizens are victims. Eveline, for example, is a girl too moribund to abandon the dust of her native city for the good air of exile; and of the partygoers in "The Dead," look less alive than the buried.

The paralysis of Joyce's Dubliners is moral, intellectual, and spiritual. In his letters, which provide excellent statements of intention, Joyce calls his book a chapter of the "moral history" of his country and a first step toward its "spiritual liberation." An agent of "civilisation," Dubliners affords his countrymen "one good look at themselves" in a "nicely polished looking-glass"; and the mirrors of literary tradition, we

* Reprinted from A Reader's Guide to James Joyce by William York Tindall, by permission of Farrar, Straus & Company, Inc. Copyright © 1959 by William York Tindall.

recall, are moral devices. Since Joyce was defending his book against
the objections of publisher and printer, these letters may exaggerate a
little; but it is plain from the text itself that Joyce's aim was moral.
Publishers and printers, however, unable to perceive embodied aim
and indifferent to his letters, maintained their objections to the immorality of such stories as "An Encounter" and "Two Gallants." With
somewhat more justification, they also objected to the indecency of
Joyce's diction, to "bloody," for example, a word, harmless to Americans,
that leaves no Briton undismayed. Indecency, to be sure, is not the same
as immorality. Whatever concerns our fundamental attitudes toward
man is the area of morality, whereas decency, temporal and social, is
a matter of decorum. Some of the most moral works—those of Rabelais,
Moses, and Chaucer—are indecent here and there. Joyce's work, though
as moral as he claimed it to be, is often indecent; yet he defended himself
against this charge too: "I have written nothing whatever indecent in
Dubliners."[1] Immoral would have been the just word here.

Paralysis is moral and central. The moral center of *Dubliners*,
however, is not paralysis alone but the revelation of paralysis to its
victims. Coming to awareness or self-realization marks the climax of
these stories or of most at least; for knowing oneself, as the Greeks
knew, is a basis of morality if not the thing itself. The little boy of "An
Encounter" and "Araby" comes to such knowledge; the coming to
awareness of Little Chandler and James Duffy is far bitterer and more
terrible because longer delayed; and the self-realization of Gabriel, the
bitterest and most comprehensive of all, is not only the point and climax
of "The Dead" but of *Dubliners*. When Joyce's heroes realize their
condition, we too, if alert and sensitive, become aware of a condition
so general that we cannot have escaped it entirely. The revelation of
Dublin to its citizens and of Dubliners to themselves reveals our world
and ourselves. *Dubliners* brings news to everyone today, New Yorkers
and Londoners alike. Maybe that is why Joyce's printer, preferring to
let dead things lie, was unable to recognize or confront what he was
printing. Knowing that and damning his printer's "conscience," Joyce
would not change a bloody word.

His attitude and tone may help to account for a general misunder-
standing. No longer enjoying the age of enlightenment, we expect our
moralists to be solemn. A common confusion nowadays is of the solemn
with the profound and the moral: a witty candidate for public office
seems unreliable. Serious to be sure, Joyce is hardly ever solemn. However moral the purpose revealed in his letters and his works, his works
are never didactic. As for satire, with which we feel at home when we
meet it in George Orwell, there is none of it in *Dubliners*. There is no

---

[1] For Joyce's remarks about *Dubliners* see *Letters*, pp. 55, 60–64, 70, 72–73;
Finnegans Wake, pp. 186–87 (Shem is the author).

sign here of indignation and what, we ask, is morality without this? Examining detestable things, Joyce seems detached and contemplative. His single gesture in the direction of goodness, which hides somewhere off stage, is irony; and we distrust ironists as we distrust wits. Moreover, we are puzzled by gaiety. Joyce's most serious stories are funny at times, and some, however serious and moral, are altogether hilarious. "Ivy Day" is one example of this and "Grace" another.

This quarrel of sense with feeling and tone reveals a queer mixture of attitudes toward Dublin. The reader who would fix the meanings of Dubliners must keep this mixture in mind. On the one hand Dublin is a moral and spiritual "dunghill," as Joyce once put it in a letter. On the other, the streets and houses are fascinating, if not always beautiful, and the people, whatever their defects, are eloquent and often agreeable. Joyce treats the cheap politicians of "Ivy Day" and the dubious believers of "Grace" with affection as well as contempt; and his horror is tempered with amusement. A kind of genial humanity attends his examination of all those perverts, drunks, and bullies who, after all, are not only monstrous but human and Irish. "Le problème de ma race," Joyce wrote to a French friend, "est tellement compliqué qu'on a besoin de tous les moyens d'un art élastique pour l'esquisser—sans le résoudre." (Letters, 118) The "elastic art" of Dubliners, presenting without solving, is faithful to Joyce's love and hate. Less moral indictment than distant contemplation, his book is a portrait of "dear dirty Dublin" and a compassionate vision of fallen man.[2]

To Joyce, Dubliners had a personal application which, though not our immediate concern or even our business, adds another dimension to a many-dimensioned thing and offers another way of getting at it. All but three of the stories were written in exile, and even the original three were written in contemplation of the flight that Eveline could not undertake. To Joyce, I think, Dubliners was not only moral censure, ambiguous portrait, and charitable vision, but a statement of his reasons for exile and its justification. Not only a picture of what he had escaped, the book is a picture of what, had he remained, he might have become. In this sense it is a collection of private horrors. Many of the characters are possible Joyces—Joyces who, lacking his enterprise and sharing Eveline's paralysis, have become as corrupt at their city, Joyces who might have been. Two among these frightening possibilities are named James: Father James Flynn, who is what Joyce might have been as parish priest; and James Duffy or what Joyce, confused with his brother Stanislaus, might have been as bank clerk. The green-eyed pervert of "An Encounter," Lenehan of "Two Gallants," and Hynes of "Ivy Day" are projections of parts and potentialities of their creator. But

---

[2] "Dear dirty Dublin," a phrase from Lady Morgan's Journals, appears throughout Finnegans Wake to suggest Joyce's divided feeling.

the principal portrait of Joyce as moribund Dubliner is Gabriel Conroy of "The Dead," who is what Joyce, married to Gretta-Nora, might have become had he stayed to teach at his University and had he continued to write reviews for the *Daily Express*. Whatever his feeling for Dublin and whatever its complexity, Joyce felt safer away, contemplating his favorite city at a suitable distance. Such distancing proved necessary for life as well as art.

Let us now consider art under its aspects of wholeness and harmony. The question is whether *Dubliners* is fifteen separate things or a single thing that deserves the name of book. We have seen that common themes assure a kind of coherence or togetherness (a word that George Meredith, D. H. Lawrence, and *McCall's* have made respectable). Parts serving the same purpose are parallel at least to one another; and variations on a theme are among the most traditional, if not the tightest, structures. We may grant that much unity, but what about sequence? How within this whole are fifteen parts arranged? Does the first precede the second, the penultimate the ultimate, and the sixth the seventh by accident or design? Could they be arranged in another pattern, if indeed there is pattern at all, without violence to the whole? These are pleasing questions, and though questions are more profitable than answers in matters of this kind, let us survey hypotheses, of which there are an abundance and a variety.

We used to think the thirty-six poems of *Chamber Music* thirty-six trivial and separate lyrics. Now it is plain that these poems, filled with meaning, compose a logical sequence, a narrative, and a suite of moods. It seems likely that *Dubliners*, commenced shortly after the last poems of *Chamber Music*, is as carefully composed—if not more carefully; for Joyce's progress was from the relatively simple to the unmistakably complex. The letters give little help here. One implies a design from which nothing could be omitted and another, offering the omission of several parts, seems a denial of order. Knowing Joyce, however, we may assume a structure. "I have written my book with considerable care," he said, "in accordance with . . . the classical tradition of my art." (*Letters*, 60) And in another letter he spoke of elements that "rivet the book together" without telling what they are.

That much for preparation, this for hypotheses themselves. The first of the three principal guesses is that the fifteen stories proceed from the individual to the general and from youth to an approximation of maturity by degrees. The opening stories are obviously of youth in Dublin, the others, advancing in time and expanding in scope, concern. the middle years of the characters and their social, political, or religious affairs. The next guess is that since *Ulysses* is a parody of Homer's *Odyssey*, *Dubliners* must be one too. According to this hypothesis, the first story shows Telemachus hunting a father and the last the slaughter of suitors. This retroactive hypothesis, now hovering above the text and now descending, demands more ingenuity than the first but is no more certain. The third guess is that since Joyce was a Catholic, however heretical, he must have used the seven deadly sins for frame. A difficulty is that fifteen stories are hard to fit with seven sins; but if we add the virtues, natural and theological, our mystical mathematics can come out right with the aid of ingenuity. This guess is no less accordant with the text than the others. Certainly these stories are about pride, sloth, envy, rage, gluttony, lust, and covetousness; but since several of the deadly seven appear in each story and virtues are rarely more than implicit, it is hard to establish a moral sequence. Whether we accept the temporal, the Homeric, or the moral hypothesis, or, rejecting all, keep on looking, it is fairly clear that some kind of structure assures harmony. It is clear, as well, that although we know a thing or two about *Dubliners,* we know little yet.

There is little agreement among answers to questions of kind and method. Some think the stories naturalistic, some think them symbolist, and others, sitting on a critical fence, look both ways. Each opinion or position has something to commend it. Edmund Wilson, long ago in *Axel's Castle,* found *Dubliners* "a straight work of Naturalistic fiction," different in every way from symbolist *Ulysses.* At the other extreme, recent critics have found the stories symbolist or symbolist in tendency. By naturalism critics mean objective, straightforward work, abounding in external details, and scientifically ordered by the laws of heredity, environment, and gravity. They think of Zola when applying the term or else of Maupassant. By the term symbolist critics mean many things since no term is less certain than this; but most would agree that external details in a symbolist work are there not for their own sake or to demonstrate a scientific point but to embody and suggest something else, preferably a moral or spiritual condition too general, vague, or slippery for tweezer or caliper. The scalpel, too, could adorn this metaphor; for naturalists often put what they called "slices of life" on their microscopic slides. These slices were commonly revolting, at best disagreeable.

Filled as they are with external detail, the stories of *Dubliners* or several at least look straightforward and, if not scientific, objective. Consider "Two Gallants," "Counterparts," and "The Boarding House." If not slices, what shape do they have at all? Some of Joyce's letters lend support to the naturalistic faction. In one Joyce observed that "the odour of ashpits and old weeds and offal hangs round my stories." In another he allowed that at first glance his stories are "somewhat bitter and sordid." (*Letters,* 64, 70) The bitter, the sordid, and stinks of all descriptions, after all, are what we expect of a naturalist. Joyce, who commanded every manner, deliberately chose for *Dubliners* what he called a style of "scrupulous meanness." Surely a style like that is suitable for scientists or even pseudo-scientists like Zola and his rout.

The symbolist faction finds comfort in the images, rhythms, and suggestive actions of *Dubliners*, forgetting that Zola was as good a symbolist as any. The external things of Joyce's sordid and discouraging stories, this faction holds, are other things entirely, there only to disclose or shadow forth one knows not what. Baudelaire, who used the sordid details of Paris streets (the great originals of Eliot's cigar butts and "female smells") for spiritual revelation, seems Joyce's ancestor. Flaubert, whose flower pots and bourgeois furnishings are spiritual revelations, seems another. Both images and sometimes, as in "The Dead," the elaborate recurrence of images in the manner of Wagnerian *leitmotiv*, establish Joyce's musical and suggestive capacity.[3] Music and suggestion are the marks of symbolists. Joyce runs, therefore, with Mallarmé and his rout.

Symbolists find encouragement in the famous theory of epiphany. Like the "objective correlative" or "inscape" or "the destructive element," the term epiphany is useful, centering our sensibilities while displaying them. Not only a respectable word, however, epiphany fits *Dubliners* and, as many have pointed out, offers another hypothesis, this time about method. Most of us owe the word less to the Church, of course, than to Dedalus himself, who employs it in *Ulysses* and expounds it in *Stephen Hero*.

While walking down the street one day, Stephen Dedalus, discouraged by those brown houses that "seem the very incarnation of Irish paralysis," hears an inane and fragmentary conversation of boy and girl on stoop. This "triviality," a detail of Dublin's streets without obvious value, makes him think of putting many such moments together in a book of "epiphanies." By this word he means "a sudden spiritual manifestation," something that random vulgarities, rising above themselves and transfigured, can yield. In such externals of the street he sees, exceeding naturalistic capacity, "the most delicate and evanescent possibilities" for the writer, who must fix them "with extreme care." The most tiresome items of Dublin's "street furniture," he says, expounding his insight to Cranly and pointing to the clock of the Ballast Office, are capable of epiphany. For Stephen, common things—to use Baudelaire's phrase—have "the expansion of infinite things" and all their radiance. Like Baudelaire, then, he thinks this world a storehouse of things as other things, seeing this or that as revelation. Involving the potency of a neutral object and the sensibility of a subject, epiphany is a transaction between object and subject that owes no less to the former than to the latter. Epiphany, he concludes, is identical with the "radiance" of the aesthetic theory he is expounding to Cranly and is to expound to Lynch in *A Portrait of the Artist*. Plainly Stephen's

[3] Many images (of light, dark, Orient, and father, for example) and many significant actions, recurring frequently, link the stories.

epiphany or radiance, a shining out or showing forth, is what we call symbolism and his radiant object a symbol.

Fussy about terms, Stephen prefers epiphany to symbol because the radiance of epiphany is ecclesiastical, that of symbol more secular nowadays, and Stephen, though far from innocent of literary tradition, is centered in the church and country he rejected. The feast of the Epiphany, which occurs on January 6, celebrates the arrival of three kings at a manger, where, though they saw nothing more than baby, saw something more. This Baby, now apprehended and showing fourth, is the radiant body. It is from this that Stephen gets his way of looking at the inconsiderable but revelatory objects of Dublin. Of the thing, made potent by insight, by wholeness, and by harmonious relation of parts, he continues: "We recognise that it is *that* thing which it is. Its soul, its whatness, leaps to us from the vestment of its appearance. The soul of the commonest object, the structure of which is so adjusted, seems to us radiant. The object achieves its epiphany." (*Stephen Hero,* 210-11, 213)

Stephen speaks of gathering some into a book; and Joyce himself made a collection of twenty-two epiphanies, some of them fragments of trivial conversation, like Stephen's sample, others dreams or prose poems. Oliver Gogarty tells how at a party Joyce would suddenly leave the room to put an epiphany down in his tablets or so Gogarty guessed. However that may be, we have the collection of twenty-two, set down from time to time between 1901 and 1904. This manuscript, now at the University of Buffalo, was published in 1956. It is less important in itself than for what it implies.

Stephen's theory and this manuscript give us a profitable way of approaching Joyce's works, all of which, as Theodore Spencer observed in his Introduction to *Stephen Hero,* may be thought of as epiphanies, *Dubliners* especially. Each story of this sequence, which Joyce commenced as he was writing the last items in that manuscript, may be thought of as a great epiphany and the container of little epiphanies, an epiphany of epiphanies. We know that Joyce, apparently regarding his collection of twenty-two fragments as a kind of storehouse of material, adapted several for his later works. What better way of conceiving *Dubliners* than as an elaborate extension of these radiant fragments, a more formidable work of the same design? According to this guess the common-place things of Dublin, becoming more than setting or example or stimulus to action, are embodiments or symbols.

QUESTIONS FOR DISCUSSION AND WRITING

1. Generalizing from your knowledge of *The Dead*, can you suggest why Tindall conditions his comment about action in the *Dubliners*? Tindall writes: "Lacking in obvious action maybe, the stories of *Dubliners* disclose human situations, moments of intensity."

2. How precise is Tindall's comment that "most of the party-goers in 'The Dead,' look less alive than the buried"?

3. While several critics cite Joyce's letter about paralysis, few cite his letter about hospitality. (Cf. Ellmann, p. 48) What is the effect of this limited citation? Tindall and others, furthermore, stress Joyce's desire to portray moral, intellectual and spiritual paralysis and at the same time emphasize his refusal to judge (cf. Stanislaus Joyce, p. 58). Is there any contradiction here? What does Tindall mean when he says, "*Dubliners* brings news to everyone today, New Yorkers and Londoners alike"?

4. Discuss Tindall's observation that "No longer enjoying the age of enlightenment, we expect our moralists to be solemn. A common confusion nowadays is of the solemn with the profound and the moral: a witty candidate for public office seems unreliable."

5. Tindall summarizes the various attempts to explain the relationship of *The Dead* to the fourteen stories preceding it. Which of the attempts to explain the unity of *Dubliners* seems most comprehensive? Which least?

6. In examining Joyce's method, Baker and Tindall lay emphasis respectively on "Ibsen's formula" and on "epiphany." What are some relationships between these concepts?

EPIPHANY*

William T. Noon, S.J.

In first introducing the *Stephen Hero* manuscript, Theodore Spencer made some important observations on epiphany, which are still valid so long as one talks about epiphany in its original, nonliterary sense: "A theory like this is not of much use to a dramatist, as Joyce seems to have realized when he first conceived of it. It is a theory which implies a lyrical rather than a dramatic view of life. It emphasizes the radiance, the effulgence, of the thing itself revealed in a special moment, an unmoving moment of time." [1] Such a theory, one might add, reflects a tendency in nineteenth-century aesthetic theory to substitute a "taste for tokens" of the sense and of the passions for the intuitions of thought. [2]

As soon as one tries to apply the theory of epiphany as a literary tool for the interpretation of Joyce's own work, the matter becomes complicated. In what sense, literary or nonliterary, should one understand "the radiant epiphany of the whole and structurally intelligible *individual* thing?" [3] Is "this thing" the poem, the story itself, or is it the evanescent experience or insight or, indeed, the trivial object which the poem or the story patterns or illuminates? Granted that the theory of epiphany has a relevance for literature, is there any good reason why if the theory is valid it should have any special relevance for Joyce? A literary application of the Joycean epiphany in its original sense of "sudden spiritual manifestation, whether in the vulgarity of

* From *Joyce and Aquinas* by William T. Noon, S.J. Reprinted by permission of Yale University Press. The Epiphanies of James Joyce incorporated in this essay are reprinted by permission of the Lockwood Memorial Library of the State University of New York at Buffalo.

[1] Theodore Spencer, "*Stephen Hero*: The Unpublished Manuscript of James Joyce's *Portrait of the Artist as a Young Man*," *Southern Review*, 7 (Summer 1941), 185–6.

[2] Cf. Gilbert and Kuhn, *A History of Esthetics*, p. 313. The authors describe the aesthetic of J. C. Hamann (1730–88) as a theory of "sense as epiphany": "Esthetic was reduced by Hamann to a commentary on the mysteries of Theophany and Incarnation."

[3] Cf. Wimsatt, "Poetry and Christian Thinking," *Thought*, 26 (Summer 1951), 223.

speech or of gesture in a memorable phase of the mind itself," [4] would seem to differ little from the literary strategy which Wordsworth described as the aim of the *Lyrical Ballads*: "to choose incidents and situations from common life, and to relate or describe them, throughout, as far as possible, in a selection of language really used by men, and, at the same time to throw over them a certain colouring of imagination, whereby ordinary things should be presented to the mind in an unusual aspect." [5]

Why even should epiphany in its later, more strictly literary meaning of a "sound sense symbol" [6] have any distinctive value as a clue to the meaning of Joyce's own works? Tindall comments, *"Ulysses* and *Finnegans Wake* are great epiphanies, disclosing their whatness and the whatness of reality. But this is only a fancier way of calling them significant forms." [7] If that is all that the theory of epiphany as symbol means, why should this theory be any more or any less relevant for Joyce than it is for any other imaginative writer—Shakespeare, Blake, Chekhov, Katherine Mansfield, to name but a few? Furthermore if modern critics are correct in reading the *Portrait* as an ironic portrayal of Stephen Dedalus, the artist *as a young man*, ought we not to take Stephen's *Portrait* theory of radiance or claritas (all, indeed, that survives in the *Portrait* of the *Stephen Hero* "epiphany") with a grain of salt? Joyce the artist need not always have agreed with Joyce the theorist, and especially when the theorist is the adolescent Stephen we should be on our guard not to identify the theory too closely with Joyce's own practical techniques in art. It may be too in Joyce's case, as in the case of other poets, like Wordsworth, Shelley, and Hopkins, who have offered theories of art or of poetry, that the works, with a certain minimum of good will, can be seen to illustrate the theories more successfully than the theories can be used to interpret the works.

The generally formless character, from a literary point of view, of the original epiphany is manifest in the example which serves to introduce the discussion of epiphanies in the *Stephen Hero* draft:

> The Young Lady—(drawling discreetly) . . . O, yes . . . I was . . . at the . . . cha . . . pel . . .
> The Young Gentleman—(inaudibly) . . . I (again inaudibly) . . . I . . .
> The Young Lady—(softly) . . . O . . . but you're . . . ve . . . ry . . . wick . . . ed. . . . [8]

That is all! However interesting this "sudden, spiritual manifestation" may have been when Joyce actually overheard it or remembered it or

[4] *Stephen Hero*, p. 211.
[5] Cf. *Preface to the Lyrical Ballads*, fifth paragraph.
[6] *Finnegans Wake*, p. 612.
[7] Tindall, *James Joyce*, p. 121.
[8] *Stephen Hero*, p. 211.

conceived it in his imagination, the literary transcription is far from significant, and the reader would not be much the wiser in spiritual insight if he counted on "the man of letters" to do no more than "record" such moments "with extreme care." [9] In order that the "epiphanic" moment of phenomenological experience may enter into poetry, the writer has no other choice than to represent the subjective experience within a symbolic structure of words. Otherwise these "most delicate and evanescent of moments" pass evanescently away, and like the "green oval leaves" Stephen Dedalus' "epiphanic records" are blown about on the winds of memory but do not exist as poems. An informing transformation of the mood through the symbolic projections of language is needed if the "sudden spiritual manifestation" is not to perish like the lost treasures of Alexandria. In poetry the conflict or drama either of mood or of spirit is seen through the language; as Joyce later on says, "The war is in words and the wood is the world." [10]

There is no exact agreement as to the actual dates of the writing of *Stephen Hero*. Spencer's investigations seem most authoritative, and though he allows wide margins (1901–06) he inclines to date the manuscript as representing the work of the years 1904–06. [11] In any case it seems certain that the epiphany incorporated into *Stephen Hero* was composed subsequently to, if not lifted from, a series of similar "plotless sketches, flashes of life, manifestations of mood and place" which Gorman describes as having been written by Joyce in Paris as "the major labour of this green season of his career" between December, 1902, and April 1903. [12] To fifteen of these extant sketches Joyce himself gave the title "Epiphanies." There may have been more. These fifteen epiphanies, as well as seven other brief descriptions similar in style to the epiphanies, are written out neatly in Joyce's own hand on twenty-two separate foolscap sheets and form part of the Joyce Paris Library now in the Lockwood Memorial Library of the University of Buffalo.

The collection shows how admirably sensitive Joyce already was to "the single word that tells the whole story," to "the simple gesture that reveals a complex state of relationships." [13] But the symbolic representation of these emblematic, "epiphanic" moments although hinting at a story does not really tell one, and the complexity in human rela-

[9] Ibid.
[10] *Finnegans Wake*, p. 98.
[11] Intro. to *Stephen Hero*, p. 9.
[12] Cf. Gorman, *James Joyce*, p. 92; see also Slocum and Cahoon, *Joyce Bibliography*, p. 153, E, 11, a, x. Cf. also "Notes et rêves," translations of three of Joyce's epiphanies by André du Bouchet in the review *84* (Paris), No. 12 (Nov. 1949), pp. 477–9. Slocum and Cahoon note on page 114 of their bibliography that the third of these epiphanies has not been identified.
[13] Cf. Levin, *James Joyce*, p. 28.

tionships, suggested as it may be, finds little corresponding echo in a complexity of verbal reconstruction or in a patterned "re-presentation" of insight. They are not without a delicate irony, however, and show already the solicitude for verbal compression and the economy of explicit comment which is characteristic of Joyce's mature work. The following two epiphanies are typical of the strategy of all, and have besides an autobiographical note which adds a special interest:

1.   (Dublin: in the National Library)
          Skeffington—I was sorry to hear of
the death of your brother . . . sorry we didn't know
in time . . . to have been at the funeral . . .
          Joyce—O, he was very young . . . a boy . . .
          Skeffington—Still . . . it hurts. . . .
2.   (Dublin: on Mountjoy Square)
          Joyce—(concludes) . . . That'll be
forty thousand pounds.
          Aunt Lillie—(titters) . . . O laws!
. . . I was like that too . . . when I was a girl I was
sure I'd marry a lord . . . or something. . . .
          Joyce—(thinks) . . . Is it possible
she's comparing herself with me?

One further example may be worth quoting since it suggests so well the manifold possibilities of further verbal growth in narrative symbolization which may be contained if only in a tiny literary seed:

                              (Dublin: at Sheehy's
                              Belvedere Place)
          O'Reilly—(with developing seriousness)
. . . Now it's my turn, I suppose . . . (quite seriously)
. . . Who is your favourite poet?

          (a pause)
Hanna Sheehy— . . . German?
O'Reilly— . . . Yes.
          (a hush)
Hanna Sheehy— . . . I think . . . Goethe. . . .[14]

Whatever may be the latent possibilities of dramatic narrative completion, is not the story as it stands more of an evocative cue to emotion than a dramatic narration? Joyce would seem to have sensed this: to have realized that his flair for the epiphany techniques was better adapted for the lyrical gesture than for the narrative or dramatic repro-

---

[14] For permission to quote these Epiphanies (unpublished as this book goes to press), I am grateful to O. A. Silverman, who has prepared the introduction and notes to *James Joyce: The Epiphanies*, to be published by the Lockwood Memorial Library, 1956. The quoted Epiphanies are numbered 4, 9, and 21 in the Silverman text. Except for my reading of *laws* for *laus* in my second quotation, our interpretation of Joyce's early handwriting agrees. (Owing to his progressive loss of vision, Joyce's handwriting becomes increasingly difficult to decipher as he grows older.)

jection of imaginatively formed reality. In any case every epiphany of literature needs words, not just stage directions, parentheses, and dots and dashes. Joyce's next serious endeavor was not yet *Dubliners* but the poems which were later published together in *Chamber Music* in 1909. Many of these poems appeared separately in various English and Irish periodicals several years before the initial publication of *Chamber Music,* some of them as early as 1904.[15] The composition of the poems must have overlapped, however, with the writing of *Dubliners,* since, as Padraic Colum points out, this book of stories was completed and first accepted for publication about 1905.[16] The composition of the *Chamber Music* poems—lyrics for music, as their title suggests—was done on the Elizabethan models, especially Ben Jonson, whom Joyce revered and whom he studied with unusual care.[17] In this way he must have been compelled to focus his attention in writing upon the objective reality of *verbal* imagery, and to notice the richness and complexity in interpreting experience which can be achieved through the artful alchemy of "metaphor, anithesis, and energy." . . .

. . . .

Between the half-wordless and largely parenthetical transcriptions of Joyce's earliest Epiphanies, and the highly compressed, many-visioned verbal formulations of the *Wake,* a complicated series of linguistic experiments was to take place. From *Dubliners* onward, Joyce's style shows a steady development in the direction of symbolic verbal notation. Levin has compared *Dubliners* to the collection of epiphanies which Stephen, as he walked along the beach in *Ulysses,* had lost hope of ever recording in words. The fact that Joyce succeeded in recording some of them in *Dubliners* is a sign that Joyce had come to see that the "sudden spiritual manifestation" was not in itself enough to constitute a poem or a story. The radiant structure of the object in literature is not self-adjusting. Only insofar as the poet or storyteller can turn the symbolic resources of his language to advantage will the literary experience "epiphanize," "seem to us radiant." [18] If *Dubliners* is the turning point in Joyce's attitude toward the epiphany, it appears reasonable to assume that his independent study of Aquinas during the period when he was writing these stories would have been one of the influences inclining him to a higher degree of symbolization in his art. . . .

The . . . symbolic technique accounts for the "radiant epiphany" of meaning which accompanies the snow image at the conclusion of the last and longest of the *Dubliners* stories, "The Dead": "His soul swooned slowly as he heard the snow falling, faintly through the

---

[15] Cf. Slocum and Cahoon, *Joyce Bibliography,* p. 93, C, 36, 27, 28.
[16] Cf. Intro. to *Dubliners,* p. v. [Modern Library edition, Ed.]
[17] Cf. Gorman, *James Joyce,* pp. 94–5.
[18] *Stephen Hero,* p. 213.

universe and faintly falling, like the descent of their last end, upon all the living and the dead." [19] Gabriel's own sudden spiritual illumination is represented as having taken place in silence several moments before the story closes. It is the moment when the full impact of Gretta's disclosure of her secret strikes him: in the light of this long hidden love of hers for the poor youth of the gasworks—"I think he died for me"— Gabriel sees his wife as a person in a way he had never been capable of seeing her before. The revelation humiliates him but does not make him resentful. Gabriel's moment of epiphany is that "most delicate and evanescent of moments" when his love for Gretta turns from *Eros* to *Agape*. "What is a woman standing on the stairs in the shadow, listening to distant music, a symbol of?" he had asked himself earlier. Now he knows to his sorrow: the sad and gracious memory of the romance and poetry in Gretta's life was in no way related to him.

But that silent moment of insight, so uniquely personal and shattering and generous, cannot be the epiphany of the story for anyone else but Gabriel. How does Joyce manage the epiphany, the radiant moment of insight, *for the reader,* and in what does that insight of the story as a story consist? The central clue to an answer here would seem to lie in the image of the snow. "Yes, the newspapers were right: snow was general all over Ireland." Prosaically literal as the verbal statement of Gabriel's reflection sounds, the mention of the cold, impersonal, but not implacable snow at this near-final moment of the story's utterance succeeds both in suggesting the ineffable mystery of the lonely human person and at the same time in symbolizing the transcendental unity of the dead with the living, and of all nature with all mankind.

This radiance of poetic meaning at the mention of snow is possible only in virtue of Joyce's strategic elaboration of the image from its first verbal appearance, when Gabriel is described quite casually as "scraping the snow from his goloshes," to the final reference of all, when the snow is represented as stretching out spatially, not just all over Ireland but "falling faintly through the universe," stretching back to the past and over the future, stilling the fainting heart, for snow is impartial alike to desire and regret. Between the first and the final references there is a whole series of seemingly unpremeditated snow images—"the light fringe of snow lay like a cape on the shoulders of his overcoat," "Gretta'd walk home in the snow if she were let," "the snow would be lying on the branches of the trees and forming a bright cap on the top of the Wellington Monument," and so forth. Integrated very subtly with this series of snow images are many other

---

[19] *Dubliners*, pp. 224–88 *passim*. Here I acknowledge my indebtedness to Cleanth Brooks, not only for insights of which I make use in discussing this story but for my appreciation of Joyce as one of the most significant of modern writers.

allusive verbal stratagems which half suggest snow: Gabriel tells
Gretta *coldly* that she can go to Galway herself if she likes; Aunt
Julia sings the old song, "Arrayed for the Bridal"; "My babe lies cold"
are the last words of Freddy Malins' song which Gabriel half catches
at the stairs; "It was in the winter," Gretta tells Gabriel, that Michael
Furey fell ill and died. Between the two series of remarks there is quiet
interaction, a kind of reciprocal illumination, or half-illumination of
meaning, "a structure so adjusted" that at the final mention of snow
the meaning of the story as a whole "epiphanizes," "seems to us radiant" with light.

Gabriel's story is the story of a man who has fallen ill, like
Stephen Dedalus, of one of the chief maladies of his age, the substitution
of aesthetics for religion. But Gabriel passes the crisis, gets past aestheti-
cism, and is on the road to recovery when the story is over. Stephen
Dedalus never recovers, never transcends the aesthetic Ersatz. "The
Dead," it may be worth noting, was the last of the *Dubliners* to be
written, a kind of afterthought or postscript to the original stories.
Joyce abandoned his work on *Stephen Hero* in order to write it. It
seems not unimportant to notice that Gabriel Conroy stands for Joyce
as much, if not much more, than Stephen Dedalus ever does.

QUESTIONS FOR DISCUSSION AND WRITING

1. Many of the contradictions and confusions involved in the definition
and application of the term *epiphany* are summed up in a series of questions
at the outset of this excerpt. The crucial question is this: "Granted that the
theory of epiphany has a relevance for literature, is there any good reason
why if the theory is valid it should have any special relevance for Joyce?" To
put the problem another way: Why does the theory have literary relevance?
Does it apply especially to Joyce—rather than to Wordsworth, for example?

2. Examine the four "epiphanies" quoted by Noon. Joyce wished with
these to render with "a single word" "the whole story," by a "simple gesture"
to reveal "a complex state of relationships." Can you suggest "the whole
story" or the "complex state" each of these epiphanies reveals?

3. In dealing with the ending of *The Dead* Noon maintains that Gabriel's
love changes from *Eros* to *Agape*. How does he support this interpretation?

4. Discuss Noon's idea of an epiphany for the character in the story
(Gabriel) and for the reader. On what basis does he distinguish such epiphanies?

JOYCE AND DISSOCIATED METAPHOR*

Frank O'Connor

Proust and Joyce were the heroes of my youth, but while Proust's
work has continued to grow on me, Joyce's has lost its charm. The
reason may be that I know too much about it. The reason for that may
be that there is far too much to know.

That weakness of Joyce's does not begin with *Finnegans Wake*.
It begins with his first book of fiction. It may be that the earlier stories
in *Dubliners* are plain sailing; to me the later ones at least are exceedingly difficult to understand, and I can only admire the critics who so
blandly profess to interpret them.

Let me begin one small detail of which I shall have more to say.
It is the first paragraph of a story called *Two Gallants,* and I merely
wish to point out that the style is unusual.

> The grey warm evening of August had descended upon the city
> and a mild warm air, a memory of summer, circulated in the streets.
> The streets, shuttered for the repose of Sunday, swarmed with a gaily
> coloured crowd. Like illumined pearls the lamps shone from the sum-
> mits of their tall poles upon the living texture below which, changing
> shape and hue, unceasingly, sent up into the warm grey evening air
> an unchanging unceasing murmur.

This beautiful paragraph, apparently modeled upon the prose of
Flaubert, has a deliberation and self-consciousness exceedingly rare
in the work of a young man and, indeed, rare in Flaubert. There is a
deliberate repetition of certain key words, sometimes with a slight
alteration of form, like "warm," "grey," "change," and "cease" which
produces a peculiar effect that is not the result of precise observation,
but of a deliberately produced hypnosis.

And here, so far as I can see, that particular experiment ceases
for the moment. But in stories like *Ivy Day in the Committee Room,
Grace,* and *The Dead*, there is a deliberate and self-conscious use of
form which produces a similar result. I have read these stories many
times, and cannot profess to understand them. I am not impressed by

* From *The Mirror in the Roadway* by Frank O'Connor. Reprinted by
permission of A. D. Peters & Co., Literary Agents.

the argument that they should be read "straight." I envy the ability of those who can read "straight" such a passage as that I have quoted, but I cannot emulate it. To me it seems queer, and I cannot help searching for the reason for its queerness.

In *Ivy Day in the Committee Room* we are in the headquarters of a candidate in a Dublin municipal election after Parnell's death. We meet the caretaker and a canvasser whose name is O'Connor and who wears a badge in Parnell's memory. The caretaker complains of his son's drinking habits. Another canvasser called Hynes appears, and they discuss the prospects of their getting paid, as well as the arrival of Edward VII on a visit to Dublin. A third canvasser called Henchy appears; Henchy has approached the candidate—a publican—for payment and had no luck. Even his request for a few bottles of stout seems to have been ignored. There is reference to the publican's father, who had kept an old-clothes shop where he had sold liquor on the side. Hynes goes out, and Henchy indignantly asks what he was doing there. His father was a decent man, but, according to Mr. Henchy, the son is not much better than an English spy. The scene is interrupted for a few moments by an unfrocked priest, Father Keon, who is looking for the publican, and then the dozen of stout arrives and the messenger boy is dispatched for a corkscrew, which he later takes back. Two fresh canvassers arrive: Mr. Crofton, a Protestant and socially a cut above the others, and Mr. Lyons, and as there is no corkscrew, two bottles of stout are put before the fire. Then, after the first cork pops, the men discuss Edward VII—a decent man who likes his glass of grog—and Parnell, till Mr. Hynes, the alleged spy, returns and a third bottle is laid on for him. Mr. Henchy, his former critic, now calls him "Joe" and asks him to recite. He recites a doggerel poem of his own in praise of the dead leader, and the third cork pops. The last lines run:

"What do you think of that, Crofton?" cried Mr. Henchy. "Isn't that fine? What?"
Mr. Crofton said it was a very fine piece of writing.

The story is remarkable for a certain apparent looseness of texture which is almost a new thing in literature. Events seem to occur merely as they would occur in everyday life; people drift in and out; there is no obvious design, and yet the story holds our attention. As a storyteller, I am impressed by the achievement, but at the same time it is clear to me that the casualness is only apparent. To begin with, the form is based upon political comment that emerges from a ground bass of booze. Everybody in the story is thinking or talking of drink, and the crisis, such as it is, when Mr. Henchy's mood mellows and he calls Hynes by his Christian name, is the result of the dozen of stout. The parallelism between King Edward and Parnell, "the Uncrowned King of Ireland," is clear, though the repeated references to "fathers"—human fathers, holy fathers, and City Fathers—I do not understand. But there are other details that show the careful structure of the story. Take, for instance, the bottles of stout. The corkscrew is absent, so one is borrowed from, and then returned to, the nearest public house, which leaves us with three bottles that must be opened by the primitive method of heating them. There is no doubt that this episode has been contrived to suggest the three volleys fired over the dead hero's grave.

The author's brother tells us that *Grace* was intended as a parody of *The Divine Comedy,* the pub representing Hell, the home Purgatory, and the church Paradise, but even this does not seem to me to explain all the peculiarities of the story, which again gives an elaborate impression of casualness. A commercial traveler falls down the steps of an underground lavatory and hurts himself. He is rescued from the police by an influential friend who then organizes a campaign to make him quit the drink, and the story ends in a Jesuit church with a businesslike sermon fit for business gentlemen like Mr. Kernan. There are two long discussions in the story, one dealing with policemen, the other with priests, and these seem to represent the temporal and spiritual powers; but even these discussions have a peculiar quality because each deals with the problem of good and bad types. Like the characters in the story, these seem to be neither very good nor very bad; and the whole manner of the story, which is the mock-heroic, seems to be a denunciation of mediocrity.

But whether or not there is a hidden structure of metaphor in the two stories I have mentioned, there is no doubt of its existence in *The Dead,* the latest to be written and the most elaborate in construction. This metaphor is unique just because it is hidden. Many nineteenth-century writers, particularly the Americans, used metaphor and allegory, but Joyce's metaphor resembles the dissociated metaphor of dreams, which is intended to baffle and deceive the conscious mind.

The story is about a young man with tuberculosis living in the west of Ireland who falls in love with a girl called Gretta. He spends one whole night outside her window, and dies soon after. Years later, at a musical party in Dublin, Gretta, now the wife of a man called Gabriel Conroy, hears the young man's favorite song, "The Lass of Aughrim," and tells her husband of the incident. Then Conroy looks out and sees the snow, death's symbol, drifting down over the city.

In the story the process of recollection is unconscious and is built up of odd scraps of metaphor. The train of allusion is fired when Conroy enters, "scraping the snow from his goloshes." He asks the maid jocularly about her wedding, and she replies bitterly that "the men that is now is only all palaver and what they can get out of you." The repudiation of the living in relation to love and marriage is an anticipation of Gabriel's own feelings at the end of the story. His aunts, the old music teachers, ask if it is true that he and Gretta are not going home to "Monkstown" for the night, and Gabriel replies that after the previous year's party Gretta had caught "cold." The reference to "a cold" is deliberate, as is, perhaps, the reference to Monkstown because the Cistercian monks mentioned later who are supposed to "sleep in their coffins" are another metaphor of death. The party is, of course, a musical one, as the young man had been a singer. Because the setting of the incident has also to be placed by means of allusion, one of the guests, Miss Ivors, who is a Nationalist, talks of going with a party to the west of Ireland during the summer, and disputes with Gabriel, who prefers to go abroad. The reference to marriage at the opening is continued by things like the old song, "Arrayed for the Bridal," and the imperfections of "the men that is now" are emphasized by the mention of Caruso, who, though he may be a good singer, is not nearly so good as a forgotten tenor named Parkinson, while in Gabriel's speech he contrasts Miss Ivors with his aunts and finds her to "lack those qualities of humanity, of hospitality, of kindly humour which belonged to an older day." His tribute to the memory of the dead is only another chord in the theme, which is simply that all love and beauty and grace are with the dead, and that as husband he himself can never compete with that long-dead youth until the snows cover himself as well.

It is a beautiful story, and perhaps here, at any rate, the mysterious effect of dissociated metaphor is not out of place, though elsewhere I find that it produces something akin to claustrophobia in me.

QUESTIONS FOR DISCUSSION AND WRITING

1. In an earlier essay W. T. Noon wrote: "In order that the 'epiphanic' moment of phenomenological experience may enter into poetry, the writer has no other choice than to represent the subjective experience within a symbolic structure of words." To what extent are O'Connor's observations about word repetitions a demonstration of "a symbolic structure of words"? Can you find any such structures in The Dead?

2. O'Connor remarks of Joyce's story, "Ivy Day in the Committee Room": "Events seem to occur merely as they would occur in everyday life; people drift in and out; there is no obvious design, and yet the story holds our attention." To what extent is this comment applicable to The Dead? Is there a lack of "obvious design" in that story? What is it about the story that holds our attention?

3. What is the "hidden structure of metaphor," or the "dissociated metaphor," which O'Connor discovers in The Dead?

4. Discuss O'Connor's summary of The Dead which begins: "The story is about a young man with tuberculosis living in the west of Ireland who falls in love with a girl called Gretta."

5. O'Connor feels that Joyce's metaphorical method can produce a feeling "akin to claustrophobia." Can you suggest some reasons why O'Connor reacts in this manner?

✿

✿

PART THREE

CRITICAL PERSPECTIVES —
FORM, THEME, SYMBOL

STAGES IN "THE DEAD"*

Kenneth Burke

Joyce's story, "The Dead" (in *Dubliners*), seems particularly to profit by a close attention to "stages." [1]

In the first of its three parts, the keynote is expectancy, which is amplified by many appropriate details: talk of preparations, arrivals, introductions, apprehensions, while fittingly the section ends on an unfinished story. All these details are in terms of everyday sociality, to do with the warming-up of the party, stressing an avid engrossment in such an order of motives, as though they were the very essence of reality. There are a few superficial references to the theme of death (the passing mention of two dead relatives who are never mentioned again, and Gabriel's remark that he had been delayed because it had taken his wife "three mortal hours" to dress). And there is one enigmatic detail, though at this stage of the story it looks wholly realistic: the reference to the snow on Gabriel's galoshes and overcoat as he enters, bringing in a "cold fragrant air from out-of-doors."

The second stage, dealing with the party at its height, could be analysed almost as a catalogue of superficial socialities, each in its way slightly false or misfit. The mood was set incipiently in the first part, when Gabriel offers the servant a tip. He had known her before she became a servant, hence his act (involving sociality of a sort) is not quite right. In the second stage, there is a welter of such intangible infelicities, as with the fact that Mary Jane's singing received the most vigorous applause from "four young men in the doorway who had gone away to the refreshment-room at the beginning of the piece but had come back when the piano has stopped." This section is a thesaurus of what we

---

* From "Three Definitions" by Kenneth Burke, *Kenyon Review*, XIII (Spring, 1951). Reprinted by permission of *Kenyon Review* and Professor Burke. Currently reprinted in *Perspectives by Incongruity* and *Terms for Order*, by Kenneth Burke, edited by Stanley Edgar Hyman, Indiana University Press.

[1] This excerpt is taken from a longer study in which Mr. Burke had already discussed Aristotle's stages, or "quantitative parts of tragedy," as given in Chapter XII of the *Poetics* (Prologue, Episode, Exode, Parode, Stasimon, Commos). He is here concerned with developing Aristotle's idea in a fresh direction.

might call "halfway" socialities, such as Miss Ivor's "propagandism" for the Irish movement (in leaving early, she cries, *"Beannacht libh"*), Freddy's drunken amiability, Gabriel's dutiful conversation with Freddy's mother, the parlor talk about music, the conviviality through common participation in the materials of the feast, Gabriel's slightly hollow after-dinner speech that was noisily acclaimed, Gabriel's distant relationship to two of the women who are giving the party, the few words with his wife indicating familiarity without intimacy, the somewhat gingerly treatment of the one Protestant among Catholics.

Such is the theme amplified, with apparent realistic engrossment, in this section. There are also a few explicit but glancing references to death. One threatens to be serious, when some of the Catholics try to tell the Protestant why certain monks sleep in their coffins; but "as the subject had grown lugubrious it was buried in a silence of the table," etc. And twice there is the enigmatic antithesis, the theme of the snow in the night, still wholly realistic in guise: "Gabriel's warm trembling fingers tapped the cold pane of the window. How cool it must be outside! How pleasant it would be to walk out alone, first along by the river and then through the park! Then snow would be lying on the branches of the trees and forming a bright cap on the top of the Wellington Monument." In the other passage, there is likewise a reference to the "gleaming cap of snow" that Gabriel associated with the Monument. (One never knows how exacting to be, when comparing such passages; yet, as regards these references to the "cap" of snow, looking back we note that, when Gabriel first entered, the light fringe of snow lay "like a cape" on his shoulders. Cap—cape. Where secret identifications are taking form, since we are in time to learn that this snow stands for some essence beyond the appearances of halfway sociality, might not the signatures mark their secret relationship thus punwise?

In any case, the third section deals with events following the party. The cycle of realistic expectations and eventualities is drawing to a close. The party breaks up. We are now free to penetrate the implications of the antithetical moment. ("How much more pleasant it would be there than at the supper table!" Gabriel had thought, in one of those two outlaw flashes when he had imagined the snow outside in the night.)

The first two sections were best described, we think, by a block-like method. Thus, for the first, we simply noted how the theme of expectancy could be stated in variation; and for the second, we broke the analysis into a list of variations on the theme of halfway sociality. For the point we were trying to make, it didn't matter in what order we listed these details. But the third section concerns initiation into a mystery. It is to take us beyond the realm of realism, as so conceived, into the realm of *ideality*. Hence, there is a strict succession of stages, in the development towards a more exacting kind of vision. Each stage is the way-in to the next, as the narrow-visioned expectations of the party had been the way-in to the disclosures following the party.

The party is over. Where will we go? Is there not a symbolism emerging in the realism, when Gabriel tells the anecdote of the old horse that went round and round the monument? Next, the topic becomes that of every-which-way (we are still undecided), as the cabman is given conflicting directions by different members of the party. "The confusion grew greater and the cabman was directed differently by Freddy Malins and Mr. Browne, each of whom had his head out through a window of the cab. The difficulty was to know where to drop Mr. Browne along the route, and Aunt Kate, Aunt Julia and Mary Jane helped the discussion from the doorstep with cross-directions and contradictions and abundance of laughter." Finally, "the horse was whipped up and the cab rattled off along the quay amid a chorus of laughter and adieus." We are en route, so far as realistic topics are concerned. But Gabriel and his wife have not yet left. And the development from now on is to concern them. Tableau: A man is singing; Gabriel's wife, Gretta, is listening attentively, standing on the staircase, "near the top of the first flight"; Gabriel, below, is looking up admiringly. And "he asked himself what is a woman standing on the stairs in the shadows, listening to distant music, a symbol of."

Previously we mentioned the form of the *Theaetetus:* how every time Socrates had brought things to an apparently satisfactory close, each such landing-place was found to be but the occasion for a new flight, a new search, that first seemed like an arrival, then opened up a new disclosure in turn. We believe that the remainder of this story possesses "dialectical form" in much that same sense. You might even call it the narrative equivalent of a Platonic dialogue. For from now on, Gabriel goes through a series of disclosures. Each time, he thinks he is really close to the essence; then another consideration emerges, that requires him to move on again. Let's be as bluntly schematic as possible. It is not our job to regive the quality of the story; for that, one should go to the story itself. The stages, schematized, are these:

(1) As against the familiar but not intimate relations we have already seen, between Gabriel and his wife, here is a new motive; Gabriel sees "grace and mystery in her attitude as if she were a symbol of something." And later, just before she asks the name of the song, at the sight of her flushed cheeks and shining eyes "a sudden tide of joy went leaping out of his heart."

(2) They had arranged to spend the night in a nearby hotel. Hence, passages to suggest that he is recovering some of the emotions he had felt at the time of their honeymoon. ("Their children, his writing, her household cares had not quenched all their souls' tender fire," a reflection growing out of realistic reference to a literal fire.)

(3) Crossing a bridge, amid talk of the snow on the statue, while "Gabriel was again in a cab with her, galloping to catch the boat, galloping to their honeymoon."

(4) Building up the sense of Gabriel's possessiveness ("happy that she

was his, proud of her grace and wifely carriage . . . a keen pang of lust
. . . a new adventure," etc.).

(5) But, after the porter has assigned them to their room and left, the
moment does not seem right. Gabriel's irritation.

(6) She kisses him, calls him "a generous person." His self-satisfaction.
"Now that she had fallen to him so easily, he wondered why he had
been so diffident."

(7) Then the disclosures begin. He finds that he has misgauged everything. She has been thinking of that song. (Gabriel sees himself in the
mirror).

(8) At first taken aback, he next recovers his gentleness, then makes
further inquiries. Angry, he learns that the song reminds her of a boy,
Michael Furey, who used to sing the song. His jealousy. (Thus, up to
now, each step nearer to her had been but the preparation for a more
accurate sense of their separation.)

(9) On further inquiry, he learns of the boy's frail love for her. "I think
he died for me," Gretta said, whereat "A vague terror seized Gabriel at
this answer, as if, at that hour when he had hoped to triumph, some
impalpable and vindictive being was coming against him, gathering
forces against him in its vague world."[2] He died for her? Died that
something might live? It is an arresting possibility.

(10) After telling of this adolescent attachment, she cries herself to
sleep.

So, we have narrowed things down, from all the party, to Gabriel
and Gretta, and now to Gabriel alone. The next two pages or so involve
a silent discipline, while he brings himself to relinquish his last claims
upon her, as specifically his. The world of conditions is now to be transcended. Gretta had called him "generous," in a passage that Gabriel had
misgauged. Now we learn that "generous tears filled Gabriel's eyes."
The transcending of conditions, the ideal abandoning of property, is
stated in Joyce's own words, thus: "His own identity was falling out
into a grey impalpable world: the solid world itself, which these dead
had one time reared and lived in, dissolving and dwindling." For "his
soul had approached that region where dwell the vast hosts of the dead."

Understandably, for if the world of conditions is the world of the
living, then the transcending of conditions will, by the logic of such

[2] One observer analysing the *Portrait,* noted that among the body-spirit
equations were grease and gas, grease being to body as gas is to spirit. Hence,
on learning that Michael Furey "was in the gasworks," we assume that his
spirituality is thus signalized roundabout, too. But we don't quite know what
to make of the possible relation between "Gretta" and "great" in these lines:
 ."I suppose you were in love with Michael Furey, Gretta," he said.
 "I was great with him at that time," she said.
Probably nothing should be made of it. But we do believe that such correla-
tions should be noted tentatively. For we would ask ourselves how methodic
a terminology is. Correspondences should be noted. But they should be left at
loose ends, except when there are good reasons for tying such ends together.

terms, equal the world of the dead. (Or, Kant-wise, we contemplate the divine; for if God transcends nature, and nature is the world of conditions, then God is the unconditioned.)

Psychologically, there are other likely interpretations here. Gabriel, finally, loves his wife, not even in terms of his honeymoon (with its strong connotations of ownership), but through the medium of an adolescent, dead at seventeen. With this dead boy he identifies himself. Perhaps because here likewise was a kind of unconditionedness, in the Gideas sense, that all was still largely in the realm of unfulfilled possibilities, inclinations or dispositions not yet rigidified into channels? There is even the chance that, in his final yielding, his identification with the dead boy, he is meeting again his own past adolescent self, with all its range of susceptibilities surviving now only like a shade in his memory.

In any case, once we have been brought to this stage of "generosity," where Gabriel can at last arrive at the order of ideal sociality, seeing all living things in terms of it, we return to the topic of snow, which becomes the *mythic image,* in the world of conditions, standing for the transcendence above the conditioned.

> It was falling on every part of the dark central plain, on the treeless hills, falling softly upon the Bog of Allen and, farther westward, softly falling into the dark mutinous Shannon waves. It was falling, too, upon every part of the lonely churchyard on the hill where Michael Furey lay buried. It lay thickly drifted on the crooked crosses and headstones, on the spears of the little grave on the barren thorns. His soul swooned slowly as he heard the snow falling faintly through the universe and faintly falling, like the descent of their last end, upon the living and the dead.

"Upon the living and the dead." That is, upon the two as merged. That is, upon the world of conditions as seen through the spirit of conditions transcended, of ideal sociality beyond material divisiveness.

QUESTIONS FOR DISCUSSION AND WRITING

1. Burke says the first "stage" of The Dead ends "fittingly" on an unfinished story. Why do you think he feels this is a fitting way to end the section?

2. The second section, Burke feels, "could be analysed almost as a catalogue of superficial socialities." What are some of these "superficial socialities" he is referring to?

3. Comment on Burke's question: "Cap—cape. Where secret identifications are taking form, since we are in time to learn that this snow stands for some essence beyond the appearances of halfway sociality, might not the signatures mark their secret relationship thus punwise?"

4. Following Burke's argument, expand on his observation that "the third section concerns initiation into a mystery."

5. How does the principle of "sociality" unify Burke's concept of stages in The Dead?

STRUCTURE AND SYMPATHY IN
JOYCE'S "THE DEAD"*

C. C. Loomis, Jr.

James Joyce's "The Dead" culminates in Gabriel Conroy's timeless moment of almost supreme vision. The fragments of his life's experience, of the epitomizing experiences of one evening in particular, are fused together into a whole: "self-bounded and self-contained upon the immeasurable background of space and time." [1] Initiated by a moment of deep, if localized, sympathy, his vision and this sympathy expand together to include not only himself, Gretta, and his aunts, but all Ireland, and, with the words "all the living and all the dead," all humanity.

Gabriel's epiphany manifests Joyce's fundamental belief that true, objective perception will lead to true, objective sympathy; such perception and such sympathy, however, ultimately defy intellectual analysis. Joyce carefully avoids abstract definition of Gabriel's vision by embodying it within the story's central symbol: the snow, which becomes paradoxically warm in the moment of vision, through which Gabriel at long last feels the deeply unifying bond of common mortality.

Gabriel's experience is intellectual only at that level on which intellect and emotional intuition blend, and the full power of the story can be apprehended by the reader only if he sympathetically shares the experience with Gabriel. As understanding of himself, then of his world, then of humanity floods Gabriel, so understanding of Gabriel, his world, and humanity in terms of the story floods the reader. The understanding in both cases is largely emotional and intuitive; intellectual analysis of the snow symbol, however successful, leaves a large surplus of emotion unexplained.

Therefore, Joyce had to generate increasing reader-sympathy as he approached the vision, but this sympathy could not be generated by complete reader-identification with Gabriel. If the reader identifies himself unreservedly with Gabriel in the first ninety percent of the story, he will lose that critical insight into him which is necessary for full

---

[1] James Joyce, *Portrait of the Artist as a Young Man* (New York, 1928), p. 249. See also Irene Hendry, "Joyce's Epiphanies" in *Critiques and Essays on Modern Fiction*, John W. Aldridge, ed. (New York, 1952), p. 129.

* From PMLA, LXXV (March 1960), 149–151. Reprinted by permission of the Modern Language Association and the author.

apprehension of his vision. It is, after all, Gabriel's vision, and there is no little irony in this fact. The vision is in sharp contrast with his previous view of the world: in fact, it literally opens a new world to him. If the reader identifies himself uncritically with Gabriel at any point in the story, he is liable to miss those very shortcomings which make the vision meaningful. Yet, in the actual moments of vision, the reader must share Gabriel's view; in a real sense, he must identify himself with Gabriel: "feel with" him.

Joyce, therefore, had to create sympathy without encouraging the reader to a blind, uncritical identification. One aspect of his solution to this problem is a monument to his genius. In the main body of the story, while he is constantly dropping meaningful, often semi-symbolic details which deepen the gulf between the reader and Gabriel, he is also generating what can best be called "aesthetic sympathy"; by the very structure of the story, he increasingly pulls the reader into the story.

"The Dead" can be divided, not arbitrarily, into five sections: the musicale, the dinner, the farewells and the drive to the hotel, the scene between Gabriel and Gretta in their room, and, finally, the vision itself. A few of these sections are separated by a time lapse, a few flow smoothly into one another; in all cases, however, the reader is aware of a slight "shifting of gears" between sections.

These sections become shorter as the story progresses. The effect of this constant shortening of scenes, together with a constant speeding up in the narrative line, is an almost constant increase of pace. Within each of the sections, Joyce carefully builds up to a climax, then slackens the pace slightly at the beginning of the next section as he begins to build up to a new climax. The pace in the sections is progressively more rapid, however, partially because of the cumulative effect of the narrative. As the story progresses, more things happen in less time.

The effect of increasing pace is complemented and strengthened by another structural aspect of the story. As the pace increases, the focus narrows. The constantly narrowing focus and the constantly increasing pace complement one another and act to pull the reader into the story. He is caught up in a whirlpool movement, ever-narrowing, ever-faster.

There is much activity in the first part of "The Dead," but the activity is diffuse and the effect is not of great pace. We are given a slightly confused, overall picture of activity: dancing, drinking, singing, chatter. Characters are introduced one after another: Lily, Gabriel, Gretta, the Misses Morkan, Mary Jane, Mr. Browne, Freddy Malins and his mother, Miss Ivors, and so on. Our scope is broad and general. Increasingly, Gabriel becomes our mode of consciousness, but he himself cannot assimilate all the activity. He retreats, isolates himself within his deep but insecure egotism. Rationalizing that "their grade of culture differed from his," he bides his time until dinner, when he knows he will be the center of all eyes.

In this first section, it is interesting to note how Joyce gives us Gabriel's point of view without compromising his own fundamental objectivity; even though we see largely through Gabriel's "delicate and restless" eyes, we nevertheless become increasingly aware of his character, of his defensive feelings of intellectual and social superiority in particular. His eyes are offended by the glittering, waxed floors, his ears by the "indelicate clattering" of the dancers, his intellect by all those present, particularly Miss Ivors, who "has a crow to pluck" with him, and constitutes a threat to his shaky feelings of superiority. His attitude can best be summed up by his reflection, ironic and revealing in view of the toast to come, that his aunts are "only two ignorant old women." Such comments are introduced quietly, but they serve to keep the reader from identifying himself too wholeheartedly with Gabriel. We feel with him to a degree even in these early sections of the story, but our sympathy is seriously reserved and qualified.[2]

In the second section, our focus narrows to the dinner table, and to a few characters at it; the others are blurred in the background. Tension about Gabriel's toast has been built up in the first section; now the pace increases as this particular tension is relieved. The toast, hypocritical and condescending, makes us further aware of Gabriel's isolation from those around him.

The pace in this scene is considerably more rapid than in the first. It builds up to the climax, the toast, in a few brief pages; then there is a slackening with the applause and singing.

There is a time-lapse between the conclusion of the toast and the next section; Joyce seems to shift to a higher range. From this point to the moment of vision, the pace increases and the focus narrows almost geometrically.

The shouts and laughter of the departure signal the end of the party, but are counter-balanced by the fine, almost silent tableau of Gabriel watching Gretta on the staircase. Our focus is beginning to narrow down to these two main characters. Gretta has been deliberately held in the background until this moment; now she emerges.

The repeated goodnights and the noisy trip through silent, snow-blanketed Dublin are given increased pace through Gabriel's increasing lust; the pace becomes the pace of "the blood bounding along his veins" and the "thoughts rioting through his brain." The fires of this lust begin to thaw the almost life-deep frost of his self-consciousness. The superiority and self-delusion are still dominant: there is much irony in his remembering "their moments of ecstasy," for his lust is far from ecstatic love. It is, however, the first step toward the moment of objective vision.

[2] For an enlightening discussion of the problem of reader-identification and "extraordinary perspective" in 19th- and 20th-century literature, see R. W. Langbaum, *The Poetry of Experience* (New York, 1957).

We are now approaching the still center of the increasingly rapid, increasingly narrow whirlpool. The scene in the hotel room between Gabriel and Gretta takes up only a few brief minutes, but in these minutes much happens. Gabriel "discovers" Gretta: suddenly she becomes more than a mere appendage to his ego. He discovers himself, in a mirror. His lust turns to anger, then his anger to humility. Gretta, caught up in her memories of the "boy in the gasworks," Michael Furey, is not even aware of his presence. "A shameful consciousness of his own person assailed him. He saw himself as a ludicrous figure, acting as a pennyboy for his aunts, a nervous, well-meaning sentimentalist, orating to vulgarians and idealising his own clownish lusts, the pitiable fatuous fellow he had caught a glimpse of in the mirror."

The peak of intensity is reached with Gretta's "Oh, the day I heard that, that he was dead." She collapses on the bed, sobbing, and Gabriel, quietly, shyly, retires to the window. At this moment, Joyce creates another time-lapse to lead into the vision itself.

Until this moment, the pace has increased and the focus has narrowed almost constantly. Now Joyce does something remarkable and effective: he reverses the process. In doing so, he makes the structure of the story not only useful as a means of generating an "aesthetic sympathy" (perhaps "empathy" with its impersonal connotations would be a more accurate word), but also makes it reinforce the ultimate emotional-intellectual meaning of the vision itself.[3]

Pace simply ceases to exist in the vision, and, of course, this is fitting. We are in an essentially timeless world at this point; true, the vision involves time and mortality, but it is timeless time and eternal mortality, man's endless fate as man. The snow "falling faintly through the universe" measures absolute, not relative time. The impact of this sudden cessation of pace on the reader is great; in fact, it parallels the impact on Gabriel himself. With this sudden structural change, we share Gabriel's vision; we do not merely analyze it.

Gabriel's vision begins with Gretta; it is narrow in focus. The whole story has led us down to this narrow focus. Now, as he does with pace, Joyce reverses the process. As the vision progresses toward the ultimate

[3] William T. Noon, S.J., in *Joyce and Aquinas* (New Haven, 1957), pp. 84–85, places Gabriel's epiphany at "the moment when the full impact of Gretta's disclosure of her secret strikes him": before the snow image of the closing paragraphs. Father Noon separates Gabriel's moment of vision from the reader's, and seems to state that the snow image is for the reader's enlightenment, not Gabriel's. I agree with Father Noon that the reader cannot possibly apprehend the depth of Gabriel's sudden sympathy with Gretta until Joyce gives him the closing image, but I do not believe that Gabriel's own vision is complete until this final image; the epiphany begins with his sympathy for Gretta, but is not complete, because not universal, until he "heard the snow falling faintly through the universe." [The passages referred to in Father Noon's Essay appear on pp. 86–88 of this text. Ed.]

image of the snow falling through the universe, the focus broadens, from Gretta, to his aunts, to himself, to Ireland, to "the universe." Time and space are telescoped in the final words of the story: The snow falls on "all the living and all the dead."

"The Dead" follows a logical pattern; we move from the general to the particular, then to a final universal. We see Gabriel's world generally; then we focus down to the particular, and from the combination of the general and particular we are given a universal symbol in the vision itself.

The logic of "The Dead," however, is not the logic of mere intellect; it is the logic which exists on a plane where intellectual perception and emotional intuition, form and content, blend.

QUESTIONS FOR DISCUSSION AND WRITING

1. Both Burke and Loomis analyzed *The Dead* in terms of stages. Briefly account for the different divisions they find in the story.

2. Loomis states: "Gabriel's experience is intellectual only at that level on which intellect and emotional intuition blend, and the full power of the story can be apprehended by the reader only if he sympathetically shares the experience with Gabriel." Explain and expand on the principle of *sympathetically experiencing* the events which a character undergoes. Does this principle imply that a critic who is unsympathetic to Gabriel cannot fully apprehend the meaning of *The Dead*?

3. Trace in your own words Loomis's argument demonstrating that Joyce so ordered *The Dead* as to increase the reader's sympathy for Gabriel. What does Loomis mean by "pace"? How does this work into his argument for the story requiring increasing sympathy for Gabriel?

4. Loomis's explication of the final paragraphs of the story are similar to Burke's and Noon's. There are, however, some differences among these three critics. Can you distinguish their views?

MICHAEL FUREY: SYMBOL-NAME IN
JOYCE'S "THE DEAD"*

George Knox

The name Michael Furey in Joyce's "The Dead" is a complex semantic aspect of the story, suggesting an interaction of Biblical-Classical worlds. R. Levin and C. Shattuck show how individual stories in *Dubliners* are integrated by a pattern of correspondences with books in the *Odyssey* ("The Dead": Bks. XX-XXII); B. Ghiselin shows *Dubliners* to be separate histories in a downward spiritual career of the Irish soul. Kenneth Burke shows how "The Dead" moves to a transcendent level of "ideal sociality," snow becoming a mythic image of purification and communion. Most recently, R. Ellman traced the biographical backgrounds: Michael Furey as Michael (Sonny) Bodkin and Gretta Conroy as Nora Barnacle, Joyce's wife. I wish to extrapolate, tentatively, certain latencies in the name, Michael Furey, and comment on his role.

The two prongs constantly penetrate the dramatic foreground and at the end hold the Hebraic-Christian: Classical-Pagan meanings together. First, the name suggests the Furies (Erinyes) and the Archangel Michael. Like the Furies, he emerges from the grave, from darkness, from Earth. He is, like the Furies, a power of Night. Should one object that the Furies are female, it can be said that Michael Furey, as memory and spirit, is subsumed in the identity of Gretta. She carries within her past the epiphany that so transforms Gabriel. Like the Erinyes, he antedates the Olympian Gods (modern Irish secular pieties) of Gabriel Conroy's world. In a sense he "protects" Gretta, brings the proud husband low, and becomes the Eumenides.

As "avenger" and transformer Michael Furey semantically incarnates some definite meanings, although some are only hints. One might consider him symbolic of the spiritual past of Ireland, for indeed Irish nationalist and religious passions figure strongly in the action and characterization. Gabriel has refused to identify himself with the patriotism of Miss Ivors, but ironically, at the end, is lifted in vision to universal brotherhood. Turning to scripture, we recall that the Archangel

* From *The Western Humanities Review*, Spring 1959. Reprinted by permission of the publisher and the author.

Gabriel tells Daniel that Michael came to help him when the Persians resisted the Jews' returning to Jerusalem. Michael is reputed apocryphally to guard the body of Eve (Gretta Conroy). St. Michael calls the dead from earth and brings the body and soul to judgment. Michael also led the victorious forces in Heaven, marking an end of one time and the beginning of another.

In the name we have clues to the eschatological power of the story. We see a final stasis, final reconciliation, and final awe as the two universes in the name collide. When first overwhelmed with the terror of his realization Gabriel feels the chill of the room:

> He stretched himself cautiously along under the sheets and lay down beside his wife. One by one, they were all becoming shades. Better pass boldly into that other world, in the full glory of some passion, than fade and wither dismally with age.

Ironically, here Gabriel is thinking of the sacrifice-death of the youthful Michael Furey and at the same time his own "death." This moment also anticipates Gabriel's final "journey." Slipping into vision, "His soul had approached that region where dwell the vast hosts of the dead. . . . The time had come for him to set out on his journey westward." Michael Furey, like the Archangel, has established in the consciousness of Gabriel, the universal "church," or New Jerusalem: "the snow falling faintly through the universe and faintly falling, like the descent of their last end, upon all the living and the dead."

Finally, vibrating between these name-poles, or prongs, is the purely Christian meaning that has been anticipated in the imagery of Gretta's story. Gretta relates to Gabriel how on the night before she left for the convent she saw Michael shivering "at the end of the garden," and how she remembered the last scene: "He was standing at the end of the wall where there was a tree." (The Archangel guards the tree of life in the Garden.) Later, when Gretta has fallen asleep, Gabriel sees "the form of the young man standing under a dripping tree." The last vision unites all the implications of the symbol-name in the mythic snow image. Michael-as-Fury has become Eumenides. Michael-as-Archangel has taken the soul and body of Gabriel to judgment. Michael-as-Christ has achieved the "end" of his sacrifice. Gretta said: "I think he died for me." In effect, he has also died for Gabriel.

At last all passion is spent. The snow is covering all.

> It was falling, too, upon every part of the lonely churchyard on the hill where Michael Furey lay buried. It lay thickly drifted on the crooked crosses and headstones, on the spears of the little gate, on the barren thorns. His soul swooned slowly as he heard the snow falling faintly through the universe and faintly falling, like the descent of their last end, upon all the living and the dead.

It is "right" that all the implications of the name should culminate in the Christian images of "crooked crosses," "spears," "barren thorns," for Gabriel is experiencing (vicariously) the crucifixion. There is perhaps another meaning in "Furey," and that is an echo of the Druid Hell, *Ifurin*, the isle of the cold land or climate. All this, and maybe more, has Michael Furey wrought in Joyce's "The Dead."

QUESTIONS FOR DISCUSSION AND WRITING

1. Which of the associations that Knox finds for the name Michael Furey do you find most convincing? Which do you find least convincing? To what extent does this discussion of the name provide for you "clues to the eschatological power of the story"?

2. How does Knox substantiate his view that the snow "unites all the implications of the symbol-name"?

ARRAYED FOR THE BRIDAL:
THE EMBODIED VISION OF "THE DEAD"*

Edward Brandabur

"The Dead" encompasses Joyce's vision in *Dubliners* of the spiritual paralysis slowly annihilating his compatriots. Although for certain critics, this story ends on a hopeful note, in my view, "The Dead" ends more conclusively than any of the other stories in a mood of softly falling desperation. . . .

Briefly, "The Dead" relates Gabriel Conroy's appearance, with his wife Gretta, at the annual New Year's party of his aunts, where, aroused by his wife as the party ends, he anticipates being alone with her in a Dublin hotel; this anticipation, however, changes to diffidence and finally to disillusionment when Gabriel learns that his wife had been recalling to mind a girlhood lover, Michael Furey, who had long ago died of pneumonia after having stayed outside her window one stormy night. . . .

Gabriel balances himself so delicately on the fine wire of his relations with other people that he expects to fall ultimately. His poise throughout the story is being continually disturbed until finally he gives in to that fall into nothingness which he had not only anticipated but, in some way, brought about. It is with relief that, in the end, Gabriel aquiesces in the descent of universal annihilation.

The incidents which most serve to convince Gabriel of what he has feared all along, are his contacts with women throughout the story, from the first unpleasant blunder with "Lily the caretaker's daughter" to the last conversation with his distracted wife, Gretta.

Gabriel's anticipation of what finally befalls him is forecast in the beginning when, in reply to Lily's question "Is it snowing again," he replies, "Yes, Lily . . . and I think we're in for a night of it." He means literally that the snow will fall all night, but he could be symbolically referring to the impending social affair of his aunts, which, for self-conscious Gabriel, is not an altogether pleasant prospect: he could be referring also to his conception of the universal fate of man, the going

* Reprinted by permission of the author. Page references in parentheses refer to this text.

into unending night after that death of the spirit which the story portrays: that he means this final thing becomes clear in the "epiphany" when Gabriel realizes that annihilation falls indeed on everyone.

On the level of his relationship with women, which seems to determine the story, it is significant that after his comment about the universal fate of man ("We're in for a night of it,") Gabriel experiences the first indication in the story of what he thinks is his own individual fate in life, which is to be the victim of the negative sensibilities of a woman. To offend Lily without seeming to mean it, is Gabriel's lot: his offense, the result of which plunges him into gloom, merits Lily's cold, universal statement about the animality of men which later Gabriel seems disposed to take personally. When he asks her if she is to be married, Lily "bitterly" replies, "The men is only all palaver and what they can get out of you." Later Gabriel feels "lust" for Gretta, a feeling of which he is ashamed when he thinks of having idealized his own "clownish lusts." The connection between his final agonized shame at the end of the story and the universal statement of Lily (the symbolically "pure" woman) is not accidental.

Having been "discomposed by Lily's bitter and sudden retort," Gabriel attempts to regain his composure by thinking of higher things: his speech, the poetry of Browning, his feeling that these would be "above his hearers." He attempts to regain his poise by transcendence: by feeling "above" the others. That this is not his true disposition, however, is indicated by his feeling that "he would fail." Failure is Gabriel's ultimate conviction, and, in terms of the story, his final end.

Having been brought down by Lily, who is beneath him, Gabriel finds it particularly unbearable to be humiliated by Miss Ivors, who, unlike anyone else in the story, is his intellectual equal. Just as Lily's retort unwittingly refers to Gabriel's lust in the end of "The Dead," so Miss Ivor's remarks disturb Gabriel's composure in the one area where he might feel secure, his intellectual superiority to the others. His encounter with her is an "ordeal which was making a blush invade his forehead." He feels that "she had tried to make him ridiculous before people, heckling him and staring at him with her rabbit's eyes." He feels, in a sense, at her mercy, and when she abruptly leaves the party, his relief is manifest in "sudden animation."

Further indication of Gabriel's feeling that he is at the mercy of women may be found in the subtle symbolic complex implicit in Joyce's description of the musicale, shortly after Gabriel's arrival. Just as in "The Sisters," the sisters offered a symbolic Mass to take over that position yielded by old Father Flynn, so in "The Dead," the sisters (particularly Julia) and Mary Jane, celebrate a kind of liturgical ceremony at which Gabriel, the victim, is an uncomfortable observer. The imagery suggests a ritual of sacrifice. For example, as she plays the piano, Mary Jane's hands are "lifted from the piano at the pauses like those of a priestess in momentary imprecation." During Mary Jane's piano playing, Gabriel's eyes wander to the pictures above the piano, both of which portray the tragic death which befell respectively victims of society and victims of a perverse authority:[1]

> Gabriel's eyes, irritated by the floor, which glittered with beeswax under the heavy chandelier, wandered to the wall above the piano. A picture of the balcony scene in *Romeo and Juliet* hung there and beside it was a picture of the two murdered princes in the Tower which Aunt Julia had worked in red, blue and brown wools when she was a girl. Probably in the school they had gone to as girls that kind of work had been taught for one year.

The irritation of Gabriel's eyes suggests his discomfort at beholding what symbolizes his own plight. That Aunt Julia worked the picture of the murdered princes links her with his victimization. This idea is re-emphasized, particularly in Gabriel's after-dinner speech when he pointedly remarks that he and the other guests have gathered around "the hospitable board [a symbolic altar] to be the "recipients—or, perhaps, I had better say, the victims—of the hospitality of certain good ladies." This remark, in the context of Gabriel's feeling victimized, is not without special irony.

The same point is suggested, finally, as Gabriel, with Gretta, ascends the stairs to their hotel room: "only the stress of his nails against the palms of his hands held the wild impulse of his body in check." The imagery, of course, suggests the victimization of Christ.

Along with the concept of Gabriel as a victim figure, Joyce presents him in the role of the obnoxiously solicitous father and husband; in fact, his family is really victimized by Gabriel. Gretta recounts his imposition of a series of discomforts on his family: she reveals her husband to be a subtle although apparently well-meaning tormentor, a revelation towards which he expresses gruff disapproval. "He's really an awful bother, what with green shades for Tom's eyes at night and making him do the dumb-bells, and forcing Eva to eat the stirabout. The poor child! And she simply hates the sight of it! . . ." Gretta says all of this in a bantering tone which does not, however, prevent Gabriel from replying to something Gretta says further on "as if he were slightly angered."

Throughout the remainder of the story, Gabriel conducts himself toward Gretta in an almost invariably cold and hostile manner. Just after his second humiliation at the hands of Miss Ivors, Gabriel reacts with particular iciness to Gretta's enthusiasm at the prospect of a trip to Galway:

[1] The image of Romeo and Juliet also foreshadows the plight of Gretta, who is doomed to be doubly unfortunate in love. It also looks forward to what Gabriel will learn later about Michael Furey.

Gretta clasped her hands excitedy and gave a little jump.

"O, do go Gabriel," she cried. "I'd love to see Galway again . . ."

"You can go if you like," said Gabriel coldly.

She looked at him for a moment, then turned to Mrs. Malins and said:

"There's a nice husband for you, Mrs. Malins."

The culmination of Gabriel's hostile attitude toward Gretta is in the room at the Hotel Gresham when, despite his apparent feeling of ardor, the tone he adopts toward her, once the door is closed, is one of "cold interrogation."

Gabriel's hostility toward Gretta, therefore, takes its cruellest form in his icy aloofness from her, an aloofness which is extremely complex: part of this complexity is in Gabriel's self-image of transcendent, angelic "purity," an image of which he could well be unaware, but which Joyce conveys nevertheless, in a number of ways. Indeed, there are indications that one of the themes in this story, a theme found in other stories as well, is that a false "purity" is destructive of one's contact with others.[2] It may well be that Joyce is hinting that Irish Catholic girls learn, as Aunt Julia did at school, in the ladylike art of embroidery, how to "murder" the male impulses of their men. The image of a young school girl sweetly embroidering the two princes murdered in the Tower is probably not without some such significance, particularly when it is accompanied by the image of Romeo and Juliet: according to this false notion of purity, death is the inevitable result of love between man and woman. In "Araby" for example, the boy must think of Mangan's sister as if she were a Madonna, and in "A Painful Cast," in which, for Duffy, friendship between men and women must be without physical contact, the male ultimately is disillusioned: in the end he gets precisely nothing out of his ephemeral desires. In "The Dead," not only does Gabriel lose his identity at last, but it is strongly implied that his own pseudo-angelic "purity" gets the better of him, and Joyce conveys this principally on the level of suggestion.

Aside from the implication of his name, we first meet Gabriel under the symbolic guise of an angel: "A light fringe of snow lay like a cape on the shoulders of his overcoat." The snow suggests wings, and subsequent imagery reinforces this suggestion of angelism. Gabriel remembers Lily when she was a child and used to sit on the "lowest step" nursing a rag doll. Because in some way Gabriel regards himself as an angel, he must see himself as in a higher order of being than others, on a higher step, as it were.[3] This implication is clearer when he confronts

---

[2] "False purity" is used here to mean a concept of purity based on a Jansenistic attitude toward the body and sex as evil and degrading rather than as goods which are to be regulated by reason according to one's state in life.

[3] In this connection it is useful to recall that, in *A Portrait*, Stephen alludes to himself in the villanelle as a "fallen seraph," the girl is like Milton's Eve to Satan, a "temptress."

the task of speaking to his low-brow audience of the higher things that he himself knows. (Significantly the higher things are not placed within a theological context, but in one of "culture," in keeping with Joyce's replacement of religion with art.)

> He was undecided about the lines from Robert Browning, for he feared they would be *above the heads* of his hearers. Some quotations that they would recognize from Shakespeare or from the Melodies would be better. The indelicate clacking of the men's heels and the shuffling of their shoes' soles reminded him that their *grade of culture* differed from his. He would only make himself ridiculous by quoting poetry to them which they could not understand. They would think he was airing his superior education. (Italics mine.)

The language of poetry is the language of angels, intelligible only among themselves: Gabriel's attitude towards language resembles that of the symbolist poets, who expected to be understood only among themselves, and among a few of the initiate, and who felt themselves isolated from society at least partially because they felt obliged to regard themselves as above it.[4] Gabriel is like the poet spoken of by the forefather of the symbolists, Baudelaire, "whose giant wings will not let him walk." [5] He walks awkwardly among those at the party because he is handicapped by angelic wings: brought down to the earth of other men at his aunt's party, he walks self-consciously among them. His stumblings are verbal, as when he says the wrong thing to Lily, the caretaker's daughter, but that is because he is attempting to speak in a tongue foreign to himself. He cannot speak to them in his own angelic language because "they could not understand. They would think he was just airing his superior education." Another indication of a split in Gabriel between angelic and human nature is that he seems to resent indications of his humanity. His physical desire for Gretta is referred to three times as lust.[6]

Finally, of course, Gabriel's angelism asserts itself in his bringing about the frustration of his "lust," for despite his apparent desire for

---

[4] Speaking of Mallarmé's refusal to make himself intelligible to the "multitude," Arthur Symons unwittingly describes also the environment of Gabriel: "who, in our time, has wrought so subtle a veil, shiny on this side, where the few are, a thick cloud on the other, where are the many?" *The Symbolist Movement in Literature* (New York, 1919), p. 182.

[5] "The Poet resembles this prince of the clouds
> [the Albatross],
Who laughs at hunters and haunts the storms;
Exiled to the ground amid the jeering pack,
His giant wings will not let him walk."
An Anthology of French Poetry, ed. by Angel Flores (New York, 1958), p. 21.

[6] "Lust" in context connotes inacceptable desires, which would seem strange since, in marriage, sexual desire is licit. However, Gabriel's desires for Gretta are allied with such a negative psychic attitude toward her as to be brutal, and, because without affection, definitely "inacceptable," which could account in part for his inhibitions.

Gretta, it is implicit both in the symbolism of the story and in certain literal details, that he does not really want a physical relation with her, or at least that he flees what he seems to want.[7] This is contrary, of course, to what happens on the surface of the story, for at first it appears that Gabriel desires his wife almost uncontrollably: "He could have flung his arms about her hips and held her still, for his arms were trembling with desire to seize her and only the stress of his nails against the palms of his hands held the wild impulse of his body in check." He is in no position here, however, to gratify his desire, for they are being conducted up the stairway to their room, by a porter. When the door is closed and they are alone, his desire subsides: he becomes "diffident" when it would have been possible to realize his desire. This is puzzling from an examination of the literal level alone; the symbolism of the story, however, more clearly indicates what is taking place.

The old porter who conducts them to their room bears a candle which here, as in "The Boarding House," has sexual significance, its flame a symbol for Gabriel's desire.[8] But it is a "guttering" candle, even while Gabriel can scarcely restrain his wild impulse on the stairway; and in front of the door to their room, the candle becomes "an unstable candle." Curiously, once they arrive inside the room, Gabriel does not permit the candle to remain, ordering it out in a somewhat patronizing way: "You may remove that handsome article, my good man." Instead, the only light he admits is a "ghastly" (ghostly) light from the gas lamp in the street.[9] The light represents Michael Furey who worked in the

[7] Gabriel's flight from involvement with Gretta could be indirectly suggested by the analogy with Bret Harte's novel *Gabriel Conroy*. In this novel, Ashley and Grace escape from their snowbound party in the high Sierras and, although they seem romantically involved, when their escape from death is assured, Ashley deviously flees the girl as soon as possible, completely abandoning her. Gerhard Frederich has pointed out that Joyce probably got the name for his character from the Harte novel, and has noted also the similarity between the famous last paragraph of "The Dead" and the first paragraph of *Gabriel Conroy*, both of which contain striking descriptions of snow. I would agree with Frederich about these two similarities; I would add, however, that there is a further resemblance between the stories in that Gabriel also "flees" Gretta, though not in a way as obvious as that in which Ashley abandons Grace. "Bret Harte as a Source for James Joyce's 'The Dead'," *PQ*, XXXIII (1954), 442–44.

[8] Elsewhere in *Dubliners*, candles and candle flames have similar erotic significance, as in "A Little Cloud," in which the name of the central character, Little Chandler, has a derisive sexual significance. In "The Boarding House" a great deal of play with lighted candles precedes the consummation of the relationship of Polly and Doran: candle flames in that story refer obviously to sexual arousal. (p. 81–82.)

[9] Brewster Ghiselin notes Gabriel's dismissal of the candle as "perhaps his wish to be lighted only by the fire of his joy." "The Unity of Joyce's *Dubliners*," *Accent*, XVI (1956), 210. This interpretation, which seems to confuse the literal and the symbolic, fails to render the story more intelligible. For one thing, Gabriel's "joy" disappears when the door is closed.

gas works and who is now dead. Symbolically, then, Gabriel has ushered his desire (represented by the candle) out of the room, and admitted the spirit of a dead rival symbolized by the ghastly light from the gas light outside. Further evidence of Michael Furey's symbolic entrance through the hotel window is seen in that later, Gabriel hears "a few light taps" on the same window pane through which the gas light comes. (p. 35.)[10] Just two pages earlier in the story Gretta has described to Gabriel the way Michael Furey, on a night many years before, had attracted her attention by tossing gravel at her window on Nun's Island.

Concomitant with the symbolic ushering in of the spirit of his rival to frustrate his own desire, is the evidence that Gabriel himself caused his wife to react as she does at the recollection of Michael Furey. In a stable marriage, the chance reminiscence of a girlhood beau occasioned by a piece of music would scarcely have caused the storm of tears expressive of a tragic state of mind. But given Gretta's point of view—having been married for years to a man who had subtly tyrannized her, ignored her, shut her out of his real inner preoccupations—the recollection of a boy who really did love her would, by contrast, have quite understandably occasioned extreme emotion. All evening at the party, Gabriel has no thought for Gretta: he ignores her dancing though she is close enough to him on the dance floor to overhear his conversation, and courtesy would have required that a husband see that his wife had a partner if he were dancing with someone else. He replies coldly to a request for a trip that would have pleased her greatly. He refuses the pudding which she was serving. He refrains from joining the table conversation with the others. On the journey to the hotel after the party, though he is happily recalling moments from their secret life together, he communicates nothing of this to her: on the contrary, he is glad of the noise of the carriage which makes conversation unnecessary. He notices that she is tired, but says nothing expressive of concern or affection. Once in the hotel room he waits hoping she will come to him; and he covers his emotional tumult by, of all things, talking about the repayment of a loan made to a friend. When she does come to him, kiss him, and compliment his generosity, it is hard to see what further reassurance Gabriel would need. Gretta has demonstrated considerable kindness in the face of her husband's outward indifference and neglect. It is understandable then that she is reduced to tears at the memory of someone who loved her with great tenderness. One can see Gabriel as a

[10] In his excellent chapter on the relation of "The Dead" to Joyce's life, Richard Ellmann suggests that the temperaments of Joyce and Gabriel are similar, among other things, in the respect that they "demand the feeling that their . . . sweethearts will deceive them with another man, as Gabriel imagines Gretta deceiving him with Michael Furey." *James Joyce* (New York, 1959), p. 49.

victim of his wife's indifference only by ignoring what Joyce has carefully made evident: that Gabriel communicates none of his ardent anticipation to his wife, but instead shows her the coldest indifference.

Thus it can justifiably be suggested that Gabriel himself causes the frustration of his relationship with his wife, and this is indicated both literally and symbolically in "The Dead;" yet he blames "some impalpable evil gathering its forces against him in its vague world," unaware that he himself has precipitated his own misfortune.

Gabriel has unconsciously frustrated his physical desire. Since the strange diffidence overtakes him before he knows of Michael Furey, it would be difficult otherwise to explain his transformation from the passionate husband to the diffident figure standing at the window wondering whether his wife will come to him. This unconscious frustration is a function of his angelism and is closely related to the subsequent realization of his insufficient love for Gretta: like his counterpart in "A Painful Case," he is a failure as a man, a failure which he defends himself against by his facade of transcendence—his self-image of angelism, though in the final analysis he cannot be said to be fully aware of it.[11]

The snow image throughout "The Dead" is a symbol for Gabriel's angelic self-image, and, in this context, for the pseudo-purity which ultimately overwhelms his spirit. It should not be thought that the snow has only this limited meaning. Rather, it most likely symbolizes a number of things at once, and is as such a further indication of Joyce's artistic complexity. There are almost as many interpretations of the snow-symbol as there have been critics of "The Dead," and it is possible to agree, to some extent, with most of them.

Brendan O Hehir, for example, writes, "the snow symbolizes death's egalitarian and pervasive presence."[12] But, contrary to this, as Richard Ellmann points out, the snow falls not simply on the living, but on the dead as well; for Ellmann, the snow represents "mutuality, a sense of the connection with one another of the living and the dead, a sense that none has his being alone."[13] For Kenneth Burke, however, the snow becomes the "mythic image, in the world of conditions, standing for the transcendence above the conditioned." The snow falls on "the world of conditions as seen through the spirit of conditions transcended, of

[11] It is impossible to avoid the idea that Gabriel is neurotic in the classic sense of one who is thoroughly self-deceived: one who brings about his own downfall in those things he seems most to want: one whose desires seem irrationally inhibited, even though they seem to be pressing to get out. "Angelism," therefore, is a kind of synonym for "neurosis." That Baudelaire's Albatross is the poet's vision of the neurotic has been pointed out to me by Mr. Howard Hart.

[12] "Structural Symbol in Joyce's 'The Dead,'" *Twentieth Century Literature*, (1957), 12. (see p. 130)

[13] *Joyce*, p. 260. (see p. 54)

ideal sociality beyond material divisiveness." [14] David Daiches sees the snow as a symbol of Gabriel's "new sense of identity with the world, of the breakdown of the circle of his egotism to allow him to become for the moment not a man different from all other men living in a world of which he alone is the center, but a willing part of the central flux of things." [15] Caroline Gordon and Allen Tate see the snow as undergoing a reversal in meaning, "from naturalistic *coldness* it develops into a symbol of warmth, of expanded consciousness; it stands for Gabriel's escape from his own ego into the larger world of humanity." [16] Brewster Ghiselin considers the snow to represent Gabriel's recognition of the unity of the fate of all the living and the dead, and as a result of this acceptance, Gabriel is "restored to the community of man." [17]

Of these opinions it is difficult to agree with that of Kenneth Burke for whom Gabriel's epiphany in the end is that of an ideal world; there seems to be no evidence for this in the story, and consequently, the snow cannot be accepted as a symbol for the "transcendence" within such an ideal world. Furthermore, it is impossible to agree with Caroline Gordon and Allen Tate, that the snow becomes a symbol of "warmth." It would seem no less logical to say that fire in the story comes to symbolize frigidity. This is not to rule out the possibility that the snow might symbolize "expanded consciousness," although these critics specify neither the subject nor the object of this "consciousness."

A further symbolic meaning of the snow relates it back to "Ivy Day in the Committee Room," in which "white" represents that spiritual annihilation which descends on the Dubliner—that gradual going forth into nothingness from being which awaits all men, and in which Gabriel acquiesces at the end. The snow falls on the living *and* the dead, so that it could well represent the annihilation *beyond* death. Of this fate Gabriel seems so convinced that he prepares for it by reclining, at the story's end, next to his wife as if he were about to become a corpse. "He stretched himself cautiously along under the sheets and lay down beside his wife."

The fear of spiritual annihilation was expressed on the first page of *Dubliners*, when the young boy feared "paralysis," although he longed "to be nearer to it and look upon its deadly work." This same fear pervades the entire collection of stories, and terminates then with the final epiphany of Gabriel. At the same time there is the closest connection between this fear and its ultimate realization, and Gabriel's complex and unpleasant relations with women throughout "The Dead." For what

[14] *Op. cit.*, p. 192. Burke means by "the transcendence" something analogous to God (see p. 99)

[15] *Op. cit.*, p. 81.

[16] *The House of Fiction* (New York, 1950), p. 282.

[17] "The Unity of Joyce's *Dubliners*," *Accent*, XVI (1956), p. 210.

he fears, in fearing annihilation, is that loss of identity in which annihilation, or coming to nothing, consists. It is in his relations with those to whom he feels inferior that Gabriel experiences the onslaught of this terrible plight: the goloshes which, as Brendan O'Hehir points out, are employed symbolically to fend off his fate, are in the end ineffectual.[18]

Since something inhibits the typical Dubliner in his pursuit of a particular good, Gabriel, like the other protagonists in Dubliners, regards the love for which he longs in some way as not good, but as evil: his paralysis, therefore, stems from aversion mingled with desire. These opposing tendencies operate against each other to cause an interior deadlock. The object of desire is felt on the conscious level to be good; but a deeper feeling causes it to be shunned. In "The Dead," Gabriel desires his wife, but frustrates his possession of her; he constructs a screen between himself and her. In "Araby" the boy seems to want a relationship with Mangan's sister, but he can only regard her projected image from behind the cold pane of glass far above the street. Eveline wants to escape her sordid life in Dublin, but is unable to pass the barrier between herself and the ship which would have taken her to a new life. In "Araby" and "Eveline" there is actually a physical barrier between what is wanted and the desire: a pane of glass, and a gate. In "The Dead" the barrier is symbolic: between Gabriel and the life of passion, which eludes him at the end, is the barrier of a grate: "He was standing with her [Gretta] in the cold, looking in through a grated window at a man making bottles in a roaring furnace. It was very cold." Fire represents passion, the cold its absence. Gabriel, surrounded by cold but observing the heat, would be symbolically looking at the warmth of life from outside, from behind a barrier. Because he has not felt the warmth of life, he must ask, annoyingly, "Is the fire hot, sir?"

The key to "The Dead," lies in Gabriel's fear of losing his identity, a fear which he courts (just as the boy in "The Sisters" fears, but is fascinated by, paralysis).[19] Gabriel attempts to fend off this loss of identity (annihilation, i.e., the loss of substantial being) throughout the story, and therefore he seeks that esteem of others which could help to give

---

[18] Brendan P. O Hehir has presented a most perceptive analysis of "The Dead," in which he writes that "goloshes are artificial, man-made defiances of nature and the elements. They typify man's prideful but puny attempts to defeat the eternal and overwhelming universe. Man must shelter himself, or at least his feet, in his overshoes; therefore Gabriel's goloshes, and not himself, most adequately symbolize opposition to the snow." (Op. cit., p. 5. Italics mine.) (O Hehir's article immediately follows: pp. 120–132)

[19] The theme of paralysis appears in this story, according to Julian B. Kaye, when Aunt Kate stoutly maintains that a tenor of her youth named Parkinson—which is also the name of a progressive paralysis—is the greatest of all singers. "The Wings of Daedalus: Two Stories in Dubliners," Modern Fiction Studies, IV (1958), 38–39.

him identity, and he reacts with great sensitivity to the actuality as well as to the anticipation of disapproval. By wearing goloshes, he fends off symbolically the feared annihilation, itself symbolized by snow. Despite Gabriel's efforts, that which he fears comes to pass. At the story's end, Gabriel feels that "his own identity was fading out into a grey impalpable world . . ." It is from this same fear of what he seems to be so deeply convinced will occur that Gabriel constructs the barrier between himself and what he wants. The barrier is a defense against failing to get what he wants.

What Gabriel fears, therefore, is realized. Perhaps because all along he was thoroughly convinced that this would happen, Gabriel masochistically brings about the final episode which disposes him for annihilation. Into his marriage he unconsciously invites from the past the ghost of Michael Furey, the memory of whose devoted love turns Gretta away from the cold rigidity of her fearful husband, plunging him into the grey impalpable world of nothingness. His fear begets that which was feared. . . .

In "The Dead," Gabriel attempts to create artificially a fictional relationship with his wife, so that during the period which leads up to their being alone in the hotel room, Gabriel thinks of Gretta as if, instead of flesh and blood, she were distilled into literature: "Moments of their secret life together burst like stars upon his memory. A heliotrope envelope was lying beside his breakfast cup and he was caressing it with his hand." The envelope is caressed—and he remembers writing to inquire of her whether "there is no *word* tender enough to be your name?" (Italics mine.)[20] Gabriel's literary sentimentalizing of their relationship represents the replacement by art of a real involvement with Gretta: by this means Gabriel, like Stephen, transcends the real problems of his own coldness and inhibition by fleeing on the wings of Daedalus, by escaping through art.[21] That his inhibitions remain, is demonstrated by his behavior in the hotel room.

[20] According to Ellmann, this expression is almost verbatim from a letter of Joyce to Nora. *Op. cit.*, p. 255.

[21] The artificiality of Gabriel's thoughts of Gretta before the events in the hotel room, their aesthetic quality as opposed to the thoughts of a real lover, was suggested to me by Mr. Robert Buttel. When, in the story, Gabriel first notices Gretta, after having ignored her through the party, he thinks of her in aesthetic terms: "If he were a painter he would paint her in that attitude. Her blue felt hat would show off the bronze of her hair against the darkness and the dark panels of her skirt would show off the light ones. *Distant Music* he would call the picture if he were a painter." (p. 26.)

At the end of *A Portrait*, Stephen rejects Emma's proffered warmth by opening "the spirtual-heroic refrigerating apparatus, invented and patented in all countries by Dante Alighieri." (p. 252). For both Gabriel and Stephen, art is an anesthesia employed to defend them from the implicitly painful commitment to real human love.

QUESTIONS FOR DISCUSSION AND WRITING

1. How does Brandabur interpret Gabriel's successive encounters with women during the course of the narrative?

2. What particular aspect of Gabriel's epiphany does Brandabur emphasize?

3. What does Brandabur mean when he says: "Lily's retort unwittingly refers to Gabriel's lust in the end of 'The Dead' "?

4. Discuss Brandabur's treatment of Gabriel's character. Give specific consideration to such observations as these: Gabriel's "nails against the palms of his hands . . . suggests the victimization of Christ," "Joyce presents him in the role of the obnoxiously solicitous father and husband," "we first meet Gabriel under the symbolic guise of an angel," Gabriel's passion.

5. Brandabur summarizes a number of views of the meaning of the snow symbol. Which of these interpretations do you find most convincing? Which least?

6. Discuss Brandabur's statement that "the key to 'The Dead' lies in Gabriel's fear of losing his identity. . . ."

STRUCTURAL SYMBOL IN JOYCE'S "THE DEAD"*

Brendan P. O Hehir

James Joyce's short story, "The Dead," is a morality play cast in the form of an Aristotelian tragedy. The question of destiny or free will is neither asked nor answered, and *hamartia* seems to coincide with sin. Joyce does not define the degree of responsibility Gabriel Conroy bears for his own guilt and therefore moral judgment must be suspended. "The Dead," as its title implies, is also a ghost story. This fact is observed by Joyce's brother Stanislaus, who classifies the story as "about ghosts: the dead who come back out of envy for the happiness of the living." [1] Such an unsympathetic judgment, if true, must be applied to ghosts more vindictive than Michael Furey's unhappy shade, though even he, in his name, seems to carry connotations of the Eumenides. But justification of these generalities must depend upon analysis of certain neglected aspects of the story.

At Gabriel Conroy's first appearance in his own person in "The Dead," on the third page of the story in the Modern Library edition, [2] his first act is to scrape the snow from his galoshes. That the snow has a symbolic value has been noted by almost every commentator upon the story, but little attention has been concentrated upon the galoshes. [3] They cannot be equated with Gabriel himself—they are "accidents" inhering in his "essence"—but, taken at face value, they are perfectly adequate symbols to countervail the snow. Galoshes exist specifically to resist

---

* From *Twentieth Century Literature*, III (April 1957), 3–13. Reprinted by permission of the publisher and the author.

[1] Stanislaus Joyce, "James Joyce: A Memoir," trans. Felix Giovanelli, *Hudson Review*, II (1950), 502.

[2] *Dubliners* (New York, 1926), p. 226. [For convenience, all further page references to *The Dead* have been made to refer to pages in this text and not to the Modern Library Edition. Ed.]

[3] Since this paper was written, a recent article has been called to my attention which establishes several points similar to those made here about the galoshes and Gabriel's mother—Morgan Blum, "The Shifting Point of View: Joyce's 'The Dead' and Gordon's 'Old Red'," *Critique* I (Minneapolis, Winter, 1956), pp. 48–49. However, I think Mr. Blum fails to make clear the dichotomy between Gabriel (and his mother) and the Misses Morkan. Gabriel himself is the sole source of denigration of his ancestry—his terming his grandfather "the old gentleman" indicates not snobbish defensiveness on his part but deference to his aunts.

snow, to protect and insulate against it. Furthermore, galoshes are artificial, manmade defiances of nature and the elements. They typify man's prideful but puny attempt to defeat the eternal and overwhelming universe. Man must shelter himself, or at least his feet, in his overshoes; therefore Gabriel's galoshes, and not himself, most adequately symbolize opposition to the snow.

But Joyce has elaborated the significance of Gabriel's galoshes into the symbolic key to his tragic position between his wife and the ghost of his mother. In the Dublin of the Conroys and the Misses Morkan galoshes are exotic importations from abroad, viewed with the same suspicion as all things continental. Gabriel's importation of galoshes—a maternally-induced characteristic—is an index of his alienation from the norms of the ambient culture.

Analysis of a passage early in the story will extricate some of the meanings tangled in association with Gabriel's galoshes.[4] Gabriel has joined his wife and his aunts upstairs, where conversation turns about his prudent plan to spend the night at the Gresham Hotel in town rather than travel home to Monkstown: "But as for Gretta there," he remarks, "she'd walk home in the snow if she were let."

Gretta's rejoinder identifies her more closely with the party of the snow, and reveals how unsympathetic she is toward his attempts to control his environment:

> "Don't mind him, Aunt Kate," she said. "He's really an awful bother, what with green shades for Tom's eyes at night and making him do the dumb-bells and forcing Eva to eat the stirabout. The poor child! And she simply hates the sight of it! . . . O, but you'll never guess what he makes me wear now!"
>
> She broke out into a peal of laughter . . .
>
> "Goloshes!" said Mrs. Conroy, "That's the latest. Whenever it's wet underfoot I must put on my goloshes. Tonight even, he wanted me to put them on, but I wouldn't. The next thing he'll buy me will be a diving suit."

Gretta would let nature take its course with her children as with the weather. Gabriel dominates what he can, and what he cannot he will shut out, by galoshes, cabs and hotel rooms. Gretta thinks his precautions absurd, but humors him when she can. However it would be too ridiculous to wear galoshes to a Christmas party—the very word suggests to her the comic dialect of a blackface minstrel show. A correct understanding of the story's unfolding requires awareness that this difference of view exists from the first between Mr. and Mrs. Conroy. The estrangement of husband and wife which, in its progress, constitutes the substratum of the plot, began, or was at least foreshadowed before

---

[4] The passage runs from page 6 (the kissing of Gabriel by his aunts) to page 7 (the interruption of the conversation by the arrival of Freddy Malins).

the opening of the story, when Gretta, at home in Monkstown, refused to wear her galoshes.

Aunt Julia represents another form of hostility to galoshes. She does not even know what they are. Aunt Kate, herself unsure, attempts, with Gretta's help, to explain. Julia learns that galoshes are "guttapercha things" that you "wear over your boots":

> "Yes," said Mrs. Conroy. "Guttapercha things. We both have a pair now. Gabriel says everyone wears them on the continent."
> "O, on the continent," murmured Aunt Julia, nodding her head slowly.

By now a number of corollaries can be deduced from the opposition of galoshes to snow. On the one hand we may read the strife of artifice against Nature, and on the other we may see the shadow of a second dichotomy: the continent against Ireland. These sets of oppositions are in interplay throughout the story, and the galoshes themselves do not entirely disappear until their final defeat by the snow. At the beginning of the third "act" of the story they reappear in their proper identity, by which phase of the tragic action the words *in his goloshes* will have come to signify *in his rash pride*.[5]

Snow and galoshes, however effectively they function as symbols, are little more than symbols. The realities behind them can be distinguished specifically only by following carefully the dramatic actions of Gabriel Conroy.

Gabriel's first contact with another person in the story is his disastrous encounter with Lily, the maid. Her bitter retort to his condescending pleasantry about marriage, and the backfire of his attempt to regain control of the situation by giving her money, force him to panicky retreat upstairs. Lily's complaint, "the men that is now is only all palaver and what they can get out of you," (p. 5) ironically paraphrases what the reader later learns about Gabriel's relationship to his wife, and may therefore subconsciously sting Gabriel's *amour propre*, but her speech has also a more overt effect. Lily's syntax and vocabulary are of a social class lower than Gabriel's, and she pronounces his last name with three syllables.

Like James Joyce, Gabriel Conroy is sensitive to sounds and words and speech. His own speech is precise, but he is not so snobbish as to be disturbed by the vulgarity of a maidservant. What disturbs him is the reminder of vulgarity's ubiquity. Ireland is unrefined, and Gabriel must constantly falsify his experience in order to forget this. Vulgarity forced upon him rips through his insulation and unnerves him until he can repair the breach. He recognizes he will not be safer among the

---

[5] By the word "act" I mean each of the three dramatic divisions of the story, the first of which ends on page 10 and the second on page 23.

company upstairs than he was with Lily—he fears the discourse he has prepared for the evening will be over the heads of his hearers:

> The indelicate clacking of the men's heels and the shuffling of their soles reminded him that their grade of culture differed from his. He would only make himself ridiculous by quoting poetry to them which they could not understand. They would think that he was airing his superior education. He would fail with them just as he had failed with the girl in the pantry. (p. 5)

Throughout "The Dead" there is a marked class-conscious awareness of speech levels. The drunken joviality of the "screwed" Freddy Malins is set off against the opaque garrulousness of his mother, who shares with him a catch in the voice and a slight stutter. The odious Mr. Brown, we are told, "assumed a very low Dublin accent so that the young ladies, with one instinct, received his speech in silence." (p. 8) Later in the evening Brown puns atrociously on his own name. Uncultivated speech surrounds Gabriel, just as does the snow, and by the end it has penetrated the obtuseness he wears like a diving suit, to drown his pride.

Early in the second "act," long before the ghost of Michael Furey has begun to stir under the moon-grey nettles and black mould of his grave, the first of the restless dead who give the story its name enters the rising action. While Mary Jane Morkan plays on the piano a difficult and unrewarding Academy piece, Gabriel, unlistening and nursing his irritations, allows his attention to drift to the pictures in the room. First he sees a representation of the balcony scene from *Romeo and Juliet*, and beside it a depiction of the murdered princes in the Tower—emblems of Love and Death, with Death coiled in the heart of Love—the major themes of the story in which he is himself an unconscious actor. A photograph of his mother is also in view. Gabriel's thoughts center on her.

The late Ellen Conroy, nee Morkan, had differed from her sisters. Aunt Kate called her "the brains carrier," but she had lacked the Morkan musical talent. She had been serious and matronly, and "very sensible of the dignity of family life." (p. 10) (Of her husband, Gabriel's father, we learn nothing but his name and place of business; "T. J. Conroy of the Port and Docks.") Ellen was the guiding hand in the upbringing of her sons, what they were today she had made them—"thanks to her, Constantine was now senior curate in Balbriggan and, thanks to her, Gabriel himself had taken his degree in the Royal University." It is also thanks to her, one may be sure, that Gabriel was able to think of his mother's sisters as "two ignorant old women," and to call Patrick Morkan, his mother's father, a "glue-boiler." It is thanks to her driving social ambition to transcend the world of the starch-mill in Back Lane and the music pupils belonging to "the better-class families on the Kingstown and Dalkey line" (p. 3) that he had acquired his breadth of view, his contacts with the continent—in short, his galoshes. Yet Gabriel was not entirely happy in remembering his mother: "A shadow passed over his face as he remembered her sullen opposition to his marriage. Some slighting phrases she had used still rankled in his memory; she had once spoken of Gretta as being country cute and that was not true of Gretta at all." (pp. 10–11)

Gabriel had been at the center of an unresolved conflict between his mother and his wife. As duty required, Gabriel sided with Gretta, and yet his mother's phrases rankled. Obviously the conflict had never been resolved. The ghost of Ellen Conroy had never ceased to insinuate that Gretta was "country cute." This accusation Gabriel could only incessantly deny, and at times, as when Gretta laughed at the urbane prudence of a civilized man, when she refused to wear her galoshes and ridiculed his, it was particularly annoying to have his mother's taunts float up again, requiring his desperate denial.

Immediately after this recollection of his mother, Gabriel encounters Molly Ivors. With his mother in the plot, the action is now fully under way. The encounter reveals more fully Gabriel's character and attitudes, and during it his self-regarding pride begins to corrupt into *hybris*.

Molly Ivors is a foil, an externalized projection of a hidden aspect of Gabriel. They are both the same age, since "they were friends of many years' standing and their careers had been parallel, first at the University and then as teachers." (p. 11) But she is a Gaelic enthusiast, he an admirer of continental literature. In every way they are antipodal and yet akin. In their quarrel he cannot get the best of her—"he could not risk a grandiose phrase with her"—and where he is perplexed and agitated, she has the last word. The occasion of the quarrel is Molly's discovery that Gabriel is the "G. C." of book reviews in the *Daily Express,* an imperialist newspaper. For this she calls him "West Briton,"—a hybrid neither truly British nor Irish. Gabriel wants to say that he places literature above politics, but his repressed political self is on Molly's side: "She had no right to call him a West Briton . . . even in joke." Molly places politics above literature, but her repressed literary self is the only one in the company capable of appreciating Gabriel's interests: "she liked [his] review immensely." Gabriel permits himself to wonder about Molly's sincerity, and half considers her one of the dead: "Had she really any life of her own behind all her propagandism?" But Molly could equally wonder if Gabriel were really alive, for there are hints that she does have a life of her own;—her "warm grasp" and firm pressing of his hand, together with her "soft friendly tone" and whispers in his ear, and all those shifts in her behavior that puzzle Gabriel, indicate that Miss Ivors feels for him a chaste passion unperceived by his dehumanized sensibilities. He does not, certainly, feel safely superior to Molly: "It unnerved him to think that she would be at the supper-table, looking up at him while he spoke with her critical quizzing eyes."

The next round of the combat goes also to Molly. Her invitation to Gabriel to come with her next summer on a trip westward to the Aran Isles is a direct challenge. The compromise of politics to literature which Molly had comprehended in the epithet "West Briton"—a compromise in itself symbolic and symptomatic of the compromises of Gabriel's life—is translated into simple terms of concrete geography. From Dublin as the center one may travel either west, to the Aran Isles, or east, to France or Belgium or Germany. Gabriel's compromises are tenable only so long as he remains unaware of them as compromises. Molly's forcing him from the middle ground unnerves him and rouses him to recklessness. When she demands of him an explanation for his choice of the eastward journey, the reply is an explosive outburst:

> "O, to tell you the truth," retorted Gabriel suddenly, "I'm sick of my own country, sick of it." (p. 12)

Twice Miss Ivors asks him why, but he remains silent. "Of course, you've no answer," she proclaims at last. And Gabriel has no answer. His difficulty lies deeper than an issue of summer holidays, or even politics—in a region of his mind he refuses to explore. A review of part of his conversation with Molly will indicate the real source of the heat in his retort. Molly's invitation to the Aran Isles had of course included Gretta:

> "It would be splendid for Gretta too if she'd come. She's from Connacht, isn't she?"
> "Her people are," said Gabriel shortly. (p. 12)

Gabriel's sharp rejoinder indicates that echoes of his mother's slighting phrases lurk within Miss Ivors' innocent question. To the suggestion that Gretta came from Connacht, Gabriel reacts as if to the accusation that she is country cute. Instinctively he denies the imputation, and separates Gretta from her countryness, conceding curtly only that "her people" may have borne the taint. Two pages later this flimsy equivocation is blown aside by Gretta herself, asserting her true nature with the frank unpremeditated devastation of a snowstorm. She wants to know what was the row Gabriel had with Molly Ivors:

> "There was no row," said Gabriel moodily, "only she wanted me to go for a trip to the west of Ireland and I said I wouldn't."
> His wife clasped her hands excitedly and gave a little jump.
> "O, do go, Gabriel," she cried. "I'd love to see Galway again." [6]

This is no simple case of husband and wife at cross purposes. Gabriel has had his face set resolutely toward the East, away from any

---

[6] Galway is the chief town of Ireland's westernmost province, Connacht, off the coast of which lie the Aran Islands. The linguistic tensions in the story are also polarized at extremes in Connacht and the continent. Gabriel travels eastward "to keep in touch with the languages"; Miss Ivors invites him westward where, she asserts, he has his "own language to keep in touch with —Irish."

acknowledgment of Gretta's countryness. Now Gretta confronts him with the ineluctable fact, and he can only respond by rejecting her: " 'You can go if you like,' said Gabriel coldly." (p. 13)

Here is the dramatic turning-point of the story. It is not merely a tiff between Gretta and Gabriel. She has forced to his attention her country origin, her western-ness, and rather than confess the fact to himself and to his dead mother, Gabriel in effect divorces his wife. This rejection is his tragic error, and Gretta herself is not unaware that she has been cut off:

> She looked at him for a moment, then turned to Mrs. Malins and said:
> "There's a nice husband for you, Mrs. Malins."

Henceforth Gretta is a free agent, owing allegiance to no one but herself. Gabriel has released her to return alone to Galway, and that is exactly what she does. Every action now will hasten Gabriel to his doom.

Unmindful of impending fate, Gabriel consoles his mind with a vision of the Wellington Monument. Although ironically capped with snow, it remains a splendid Eastern symbol. Wellington, himself a Dubliner, had made his mark to the eastward, in France and Belgium and Germany, and a grateful British nation had erected to his glory the obelisk which stood about a mile away, in plain sight of the Misses Morkans' house. Gabriel has no insight into the meaning of the snow, nor does it occur to him that Wellington's Monument is essentially no more than a tombstone. For him the monument represents an ideal serenity aloof from the vulgar turmoil of the Christmas party.[7]

As the party at the Morkans' progresses, famished hosts of the dead flock to the feast, pressing in like the shades around Odysseus. When Aunt Julia sings before dinner her old song, *Arrayed for the Bridal,* the intensity of the following applause is conditioned by the unspoken prescience that Death is soon to be her bridegroom. Later in the night, after his own calamity, Gabriel will recall this awareness: "Poor Aunt Julia! She, too, would soon be a shade . . . He had caught that haggard look upon her face for a moment when she was singing *Arrayed for the Bridal.*" (p. 34) At dinner the conversation runs, as naturally it might in Joyce's Dublin, to opera- and concert-singers. But soon in reminiscences the dead artists of the past drift, one by one, to the table. The talk then turns unaccountably to the Trappist monks of Mount Melleray, who live in unbroken silence and sleep in their coffins, to remind them, as Mary Jane puts it (anticipating the story's final sentence), "of their last end." The topic, grown lugubrious, ends at last, "buried in a silence of the table . . ." (p. 20)

---

[7] A perhaps pertinent observation is the fact that in Ireland a Wellington is also a "guttapercha thing that you wear over your boots." *Boots* are shoes, and *Wellingtons* are knee-high rubber storm-boots.

As Gabriel stands to begin the after-dinner speech that has been weighing upon his mind all evening, he turns once more for solace to a mental view of the Wellington Monument: "The Wellington Monument wore a gleaming cap of snow that flashed westward over the white field of Fifteen Acres." (p. 21) Here the monument still dominates the snow, but there is a curious juggling of perspective. Gabriel visualizes the monument at the *east* of his mental picture, since its snow-cap "flashed westward" over the Fifteen Acres, and the Wellington Monument in fact is east of the Fifteen Acres. But the monument is *west* of the Morkan house on Usher's Island, Gabriel's actual position. Therefore, in focussing his thought on his Eastern symbol, Gabriel's mind has traveled westward, past the monument, past even the white field of the Fifteen Acres, to take its view of the flashing monument from the farther western shadows.

The speech itself is interwoven with similar unconscious ironies. Gabriel had feared his talk would be over the heads of his hearers and had thought of his aunts as ignorant old women, but to score a point off Miss Ivors he determined to cater to his audience. Although his attack on Molly was pointless, since she had left before supper, the strategy made his speech immensely successful. Later Gabriel would characterize his behavior as "acting as pennyboy for his aunts . . . orating to vulgarians . . ." (p. 32), but for the present success intoxicates him. His tribute to his aunts rings with sincerity, and he delivers a panegyric upon the Irish national virtue of hospitality, which he has never found equalled in all of his experience abroad. Having told Molly Ivors he was sick of his country, he pours forth the fulsome eulogies of a patriotic orator. But even into Gabriel's toastmastership the lugubrious note of the table-talk enters, for he invokes "those dead and gone great ones whose fame the world will not willingly let die." And not only the great are dead and gone—"there are always," Gabriel continues, "in gatherings such as this sadder thoughts that will recur to our minds: thoughts of the past, of youth, of changes, of absent faces that we miss here tonight. Our path through life is strewn with many such sad memories . . ." (p. 22)

In that gathering, her thoughts of the past and of Galway freshly stirred, and with her heart saddened by her husband's rebuff, sits Gabriel's wife, Gretta. Unwittingly the melancholy words reflect the circling of her mind through thoughts of youth and changes, to sadder memories of Michael Furey. But Gabriel is oblivious of such possibilities—he goes on to homilize: "We have all of us living duties and living affections which claim, and rightly claim, our strenuous endeavors." Yet it is precisely by disowning his living duties towards Gretta, in conformity to the values of his dead mother, that he permits his wife's detached living affections to fasten upon the memory of her dead lover. His tragic failure diverts each of them from the living to the dead.

The third "act" opens as the party is breaking up. While Gretta is dressing upstairs, Gabriel tells a tale about his grandfather, "the late lamented Patrick Morkan," and his horse, Johnny. At the conclusion of his anecdote, "Gabriel paced in a circle round the hall in his goloshes amid the laughter of the others." (p. 25) Mocking thus the dead in the pride of his goloshes, Gabriel shows the first symptoms of the madness that comes from excess of pride.

Upstairs somebody is "fooling at the piano," and Gabriel, looking upward, sees a woman, his wife, "leaning on the banisters, listening." He cannot make out what she is listening to, but thinks of her as posed for a picture he would call "Distant Music,"—little suspecting how distant from him she is.[8] Gretta is listening to Bartell D'Arcy singing, in the old Irish tonality, with a voice made plaintive and hoarse by a cold, words expressing grief. What Gretta actually *hears*—distant, hoarse, wavering in the old Irish tonality—is the voice of her dead lover, Michael Furey. Even the song's words evoke him:

> O, the rain falls on my heavy locks
> And the dew wets my skin . . .

When Gretta comes downstairs Gabriel observes color on her cheeks and her eyes shining;—"a sudden tide of joy went leaping out of his heart," (p. 27)—but she does not turn towards him.

> "Mr. D'Arcy," she said, "what is the name of that song you were singing?"
> "It's called The Lass of Aughrim," said Mr. D'Arcy . . .
> "The Lass of Aughrim," she repeated. "I couldn't think of the name."

In a group of four they leave the house, and, unable to find a cab, walk eastward along the quays. Gabriel walks with Miss O'Callaghan, his mind intoxicated with thoughts of his wife. Gretta, however, walks ahead through the slush, without galoshes, alongside Bartell D'Arcy, the embodiment of her dead past. They all catch a cab at the corner of Winetavern Street, and Gabriel, in the grip of *ate* on this last trip eastward, fantasies Gretta and himself galloping to catch their honeymoon boat. In high spirits he calls a gay greeting to the ghostly snow-covered statue of Dan O'Connell. But the cab seems more akin to a hearse or a coffin than to a honeymoon coach: "the horse galloped along wearily under the murky morning sky, dragging his old rattling box after his heels." (p. 29) The horse, like all living creatures, is cumbered by the trappings of his mortality.

At the hotel, drunk with desire for Gretta, Gabriel "felt that they had escaped from their lives and duties, escaped from home and

---

[8] This scene has been analyzed by Allen Tate in "Three Commentaries: Poe, James, and Joyce," *Sewanee Review*, LVIII (1950), 1–15—later reprinted in Allen Tate and Caroline Gordon, *The House of Fiction* (New York, 1950).

friends and run away together with wild and radiant hearts to a new adventure." (p. 29) He does not realize how truly all old life has come to an end. At first he is enraged by Gretta's apparent failure to reciprocate his desire, and when finally she comes to him along the shaft of "ghastly light from the street lamp"—the only illumination of this climactic scene—he misunderstands the reality thus symbolized. He misses the point entirely when she kisses him saying, "You are a very generous person, Gabriel." (p. 31) His infatuation makes him think she is yielding until, in a burst of tears, she speaks of *The Lass of Aughrim* and of the singer who haunts her—a person she knew once in Galway. The dull anger gathering at the back of Gabriel's mind involves then more than thwarted lust. His mother's old taunt and the incident with Molly Ivors coalesce in this reminder of Gretta's girlhood. The anger grows from the fear that a vital threat may crouch in that western background he had dismissed and ignored almost out of existence: " 'Someone you were in love with?' he asked ironically." (p. 32)

In the subsequent scene occurs what Aristotle calls the Tragic Incident with Reversal of Intention. Gabriel's ironic probing, his sudden suspicion that Gretta wants to go to Galway to resume an old love affair (he so desperately wants to deny the real claims of her background that he is willing to accept a base motive for his wife's desire to revisit the west) are set off against Gretta's grieving, innocent, childlike responses. Each reply—unmeditated, unsubtle, guileless—is devastating to Gabriel's elaborate position:

> "What was he?" asked Gabriel, still ironically.
> "He was in the gasworks," she said. (p. 32)

The last twist of the knife comes when Gabriel's anger has ebbed, when his lust has cooled, and he too is sorrowful. In genuine sympathy—for Gabriel *is* a very generous person—he asks her:

> "And what did he die of so young, Gretta? Consumption, was it?"
> "I think he died for me," she answered. (p. 33)

Gretta's tale of Michael Furey flows on, in the cadences of her native rustic dialect. Gabriel no longer flinches from a syntax less cultured than his own. "I was great with him at that time," she begins, and her long revery pours slowly out:

> he was ill . . . and wouldn't be let out. . . . He was in decline, they said, or something like that. I never knew rightly. . . . We used to go out together, walking, you know, Gabriel, like the way they do in the country. He was going to study singing only for his health. . . . And when it came to the time for me to leave . . . I wouldn't be let see him so I wrote him a letter saying I . . . would be back in the summer, and hoping he would be better then. . . . Then the night before I left . . . I heard gravel thrown up against the window. The window was so wet I couldn't see, so I ran downstairs as I was and slipped out the back into the garden and there was the poor fellow at the end of the garden shivering. . . . I implored of him to go home at once and told him he

would get his death in the rain. But he said he did not want to live. I can see his eyes as well as well! He was standing at the end of the wall where there was a tree. . . . And when I was only a week in the convent he died and was buried in Oughterard, where his people came from. O, the day I heard that, that he was dead! (pp. 33–34)

Gabriel's artificial world collapses under the slow drift of Gretta's memories, and he is left alone at the end with the realities he has evaded. His pride undone, he is fallen, and is left to grope his way blindly to a new reconciliation with life—on terms much humbler than before. Gretta sobs herself to sleep, and a short time later Gabriel himself lies down unresentfully beside her: "So she had had that romance in her life: a man had died for her sake. It hardly pained him now to think how poor a part he, her husband, had played in her life." (p. 285) Looking back soberly now upon his foolhardy pride, his consciousness is filled with death. Even Gretta is touched with it: "He did not like to say even to himself that her face was no longer beautiful, but he knew that it was no longer the face for which Michael Furey had braved death." (p. 286) In his mind the ghosts gather: Patrick Morkan and his horse; poor Aunt Julia—soon, too, to be a shade—one by one they were all becoming shades. In the partial darkness the form of Michael Furey appears, standing under a dripping tree. Gabriel's soul "had approached that region where dwell the vast hosts of the dead. . . . His own identity was fading out into a grey impalpable world: the solid world itself, which these dead had at one time reared and lived in, was dissolving and dwindling." (p. 35) To his sleepy mind as he turns to watch the snow falling obliquely against the lamplight outside the window, a phrase occurs: "The time had come for him to set out on his journey westward." (p. 35)

The meaning of this "journey westward" has been adumbrated throughout the story, and yet on the literal level it has no significance at all, for Gabriel had planned no trip westward. The reference cannot possibly be to Molly Ivors' holiday trip, since that is projected for the following summer. The journey is a symbolic formulation from Gabriel's subconscious of the east-west pattern in which the activity of his life has been expressed, and marks a complete reversal of his orientation. For Gabriel the thought—one of the great elemental tropes of human experience—can only mean that the time has come for him to turn toward the setting sun, and to journey, not to the Aran Isles, but to Aran of the Saints, the Isles of the Blest in the dim Atlantic. The time has come when he must accept the fact that life is inseparable from death, when he must accept his own minuteness in the scale of eternity; when he must begin, in short, to die. The snow symbolizes death's egalitarian and pervasive presence. It falls faintly, like the descent of their last end, upon all the living and all the dead, and blots out distinctions between them. Gabriel Conroy's swooning soul follows the snow in an everwestering journey, from Wellington's Monument westward across the white field of Fifteen Acres, across Ireland's "dark central plain . . . the treeless hills . . . the Bog of Allen and, farther westward . . . the dark mutinous Shannon waves"—to the crooked crosses and headstones of the lonely churchyard on the hill where Michael Furey lies buried. (p. 35) Gabriel might have expressed the quiescence of his resolved metaphysical relationship with his wife and his wife's buried lover in the words of a poem by James Joyce, *She Weeps over Rahoon:*

> Dark too our hearts, O love, shall lie and cold
> As his sad heart has lain . . .

The story does not of course force the extreme conclusion that Gabriel Conroy dies a literal death in a room of the Gresham Hotel. He is dead, in the Christian sense only, to the World; or, in the vernacular sense of the same words, asleep. Later in the day he will rise from sleep, into a purified life, and return home with Gretta to Monkstown, where life is lived in the awareness of death. Sunset is a necessary antecedent to sunrise, and in a sense Gabriel may be identified with the sun. It is already early morning when he goes to bed and begins his journey westward, so that his mental voyage not only follows the path of the snow, but anticipates that which the sun is to follow.

Gabriel's tragic fall is essentially a fortunate one. Death is the chief problem of life and tragedy is the vicarious experience of death. With the dying hero we approach that region "where dwell the vast hosts of the dead," and with his reborn spirit we revive and put on immortality. Gabriel Conroy may have sinned and died, but he becomes, in the end, a "foenix culprit."[9]

[9] Attempts may be made (ill-advisedly, I believe) to interpret Gabriel Conroy's western journey in terms deduced from Joyce's apparent personal preference for lands east of Dublin. But a journey in one direction or the other may be inevitable—it is only the midway point, the position of the West Briton, that is untenable. The tension between east and west can never be unambiguously resolved. An interesting text for meditation in this regard is an entry reflecting many of the themes of "The Dead" in the notebook kept by Stephen Dedalus prior to his own Icarus-flight eastward to Newhaven-Dieppe-Paris (*A Portrait of the Artist as a Young Man*, Modern Library, pp. 297–298):

April 14. John Alphonsus Mulrennan has just returned from the west of Ireland. European and Asiatic papers please copy. He told us he met an old man there in a mountain cabin. Old man had red eyes and short pipe. Old man spoke Irish. Mulrennan spoke Irish. Then old man and Mulrennan spoke English. Mulrennan spoke to him about universe and stars. Old man sat, listened, smoked, spat. Then said:

—Ah, there must be terrible queer creatures at the latter end of the world.—

I fear him. I fear his redrimmed horny eyes. It is with him I must struggle all through this night till day come, till he or I lie dead, gripping him by the sinewy throat till . . . Till what? Till he yield to me? No. I mean him no harm."

QUESTIONS FOR DISCUSSION AND WRITING

1. What special significance does O Hehir find in Gabriel's galoshes? To what other symbols in the story does he relate the galoshes?

2. What are some of the speech levels O Hehir finds in *The Dead* and what significance does he attach to these levels?

3. What does O Hehir mean when he says Gabriel's "self-regarding pride begins to corrupt into *hybris*"? Also, later, when he says, "Mocking thus the dead in the pride of his galoshes, Gabriel shows the first symptoms of the madness that comes from excess of pride"?

4. According to O Hehir, what are the compromises Gabriel has made and why have these compromises remained tenable?

5. What importance does O Hehir attach to Miss Ivors' invitation to visit the west of Ireland? How is this significance extended to include Gretta? How is the east-west symbolism further extended by O Hehir to lesser areas such as Wellington's statue, and to the major event of Gabriel's "western" journey at the story's end?

6. Comment on O Hehir's idea that in the final scene between Gretta and Gabriel "occurs what Aristotle calls the Tragic Incident with Reversal of Intention."

FURTHER SUGGESTIONS FOR WRITING*

1. A score of the preceding questions in "discussions and writing" lend themselves to papers of varying length. Examine the above questions, and with the approval of your instructor, select a question for further investigation in a paper.

2. Write your own critical essay on *The Dead* in the manner of Burke, Loomis, Brandabur, or O Hehir. The major centers of dispute and the issues you will want to deal with are: the snow, the west, and Gabriel's character (especially the problem of "sympathy," cf. Loomis, pp. 106–107).

3. The student might find it enlightening to read the whole collection of stories in which *The Dead* appeared and to write a paper discussing how *The Dead* is related to the other stories in the volume. Tindall, for example, says *Dubliners* is "not only moral censure, ambiguous portrait, and charitable vision, but also a statement of reasons for exile and its justification." Compare *The Dead* with other stories in *Dubliners* in terms of this statement.

4. In a critical essay Joyce once wrote: "Ibsen's plays do not depend for their interest on the action or on the incidents. Even the characters, faultlessly drawn though they be, are not the first things in his plays. But the naked drama—either the perception of a great truth, or the opening up of a great question, or a great conflict which is almost independent of conflicting actors, and has been and is of far-reaching importance—this is what primarily merits attention." (*Critical Writing*, p. 63.) Analyze Joyce's own fiction, specifically *The Dead*, in terms of this observation.

5. Just as Baker finds correspondences between *The Dead* and Ibsen, others have found similarities between *The Dead* and parts of the *Odyssey*, and parts of *The Divine Comedy*. You might find it interesting to write an essay exploring correspondences between *The Dead* and another work. You might, e.g., examine the similarities between Joyce's treatment of Gabriel Conroy and T. S. Eliot's handling of J. Alfred Prufrock in his dramatic poem, "The Love Song of J. Alfred Prufrock."

6. David Daiches conceives of *The Dead* as a kind of demonstration of Joyce's aesthetic doctrines: " 'The Dead' is a kind of afterthought expressing indirectly Joyce's preoccupation with the question of the proper esthetic attitude. Actually, what is happening to Gabriel is that, like Stephen in the *Portrait*, he is moving from the 'lyrical' point of view, the egocentric approach which Joyce regarded as the most immature, to the 'dramatic' approach, which for Joyce was the proper esthetic approach." Making a further study of Joyce's aesthetic ideas, write an essay on *The Dead* as an example of "the proper esthetic attitude." You might wish to extend the paper by considering other stories in *Dubliners* and *The Portrait of the Artist as a Young Man*.

7. Throughout the commentaries on *The Dead* there are numerous reasons given for the title of the story. Analyze these reasons, explaining which are most convincing, which least. If possible, add new reasons why Joyce chose the title he did.

8. A fundamental problem of criticism is learning what to say and what not to say. Write an essay setting forth those things which should be said about this story, and those things that should not be said.